CW01650802

69p

Decorative Painting Using Patterns from Nature

by
Lois Brandt Phillips

Crown Publishers, Inc.
New York

To my parents and my children

© 1978 by Lois Brandt Phillips
All rights reserved. No part of this book may be reproduced or utilized in any form or by any means, electronic or mechanical, including photocopying, recording, or by any information storage and retrieval system, without permission in writing from the publisher.
Inquiries should be addressed to Crown Publishers, Inc., One Park Avenue, New York, N.Y. 10016
Printed in the United States of America
Published simultaneously in Canada by General Publishing Company Limited

Designed by Jon M. Nelson

Library of Congress Cataloging in Publication Data

Phillips, Lois Brandt.
Decorative painting using patterns from nature.

Bibliography: p.
Includes index.
1. Painting. 2. Design, Decorative—Animal forms.
3. Design, Decorative—Plant forms. I. Title.
TT385.P48 1978 745.7′2 77-19190
ISBN 0-517-53395-2
ISBN 0-517-53396-0 pbk.

Contents

1
Introduction

The patterns in this book have all been derived from the fascinating world of nature. They are meant to stimulate ideas and help you in creating your own decorative designs.

Half the fun is in searching for nature's patterns. Take a sketchbook or camera with you when you hike or camp in the woods. While you walk through open fields, along roadsides, or in your own backyard, learn to be observant. Make simple line drawings of the plants you see: leaves, seedpods, and flowers.

If it is necessary to pick a flower for drawing, one or two perfect blooms will be sufficient. You will want to ensure that the species blooms again in years to come. Keep the flower in water while you draw. When finished, place the flower between absorbent paper and weight down for pressing. I will tell you how to use pressed flowers in greeting cards.

In national and state parks it is forbidden to pick any flowers, so here you must rely upon on-the-spot sketching and photography.

Each season brings a new, rich display of patterns, shapes, and textures. As you re-create the beautiful things you observe, you will become a friend to all of Nature's family: birds and mammals, plants and trees, and you will be rewarded by gifts uniquely your own.

2

Materials

Acrylic paints were used on all the crafts throughout this book. As you will discover, they are versatile and can be applied to almost any prepared surface, whether wood, plastic, or fabric. Acrylic paint dries in minutes making it possible to progress steadily to the completion of each craft without waiting for drying periods. The paint is durable, resists fading and cracking, and is waterproof—a boon when used on kitchen articles!

There are many brands of acrylic paint on the market; two excellent ones are Hyplar and Liquitex. I find these two brands compatible when mixed together, but there are some brands of acrylic that cannot be intermixed successfully.

There are dozens of colors and shades to choose from, but you can begin with just a few basic colors:

Titanium white	Yellow ocher
Cadmium red medium	Ivory black
Cadmium yellow medium	Cadmium orange
	Burnt umber
Phthalocyanine (thalo) blue	Thalo green
	Burnt sienna

Acrylic brushes and bristle brushes are recommended; those of sable are not firm enough for most of the crafts. Some useful sizes in brushes are:

Flat 2″ acrylic brush for applying base coats, varnish, or gesso
Round white bristle, sizes 1 and 2
Acrylic brushes, flat sizes 1, 2, and 5

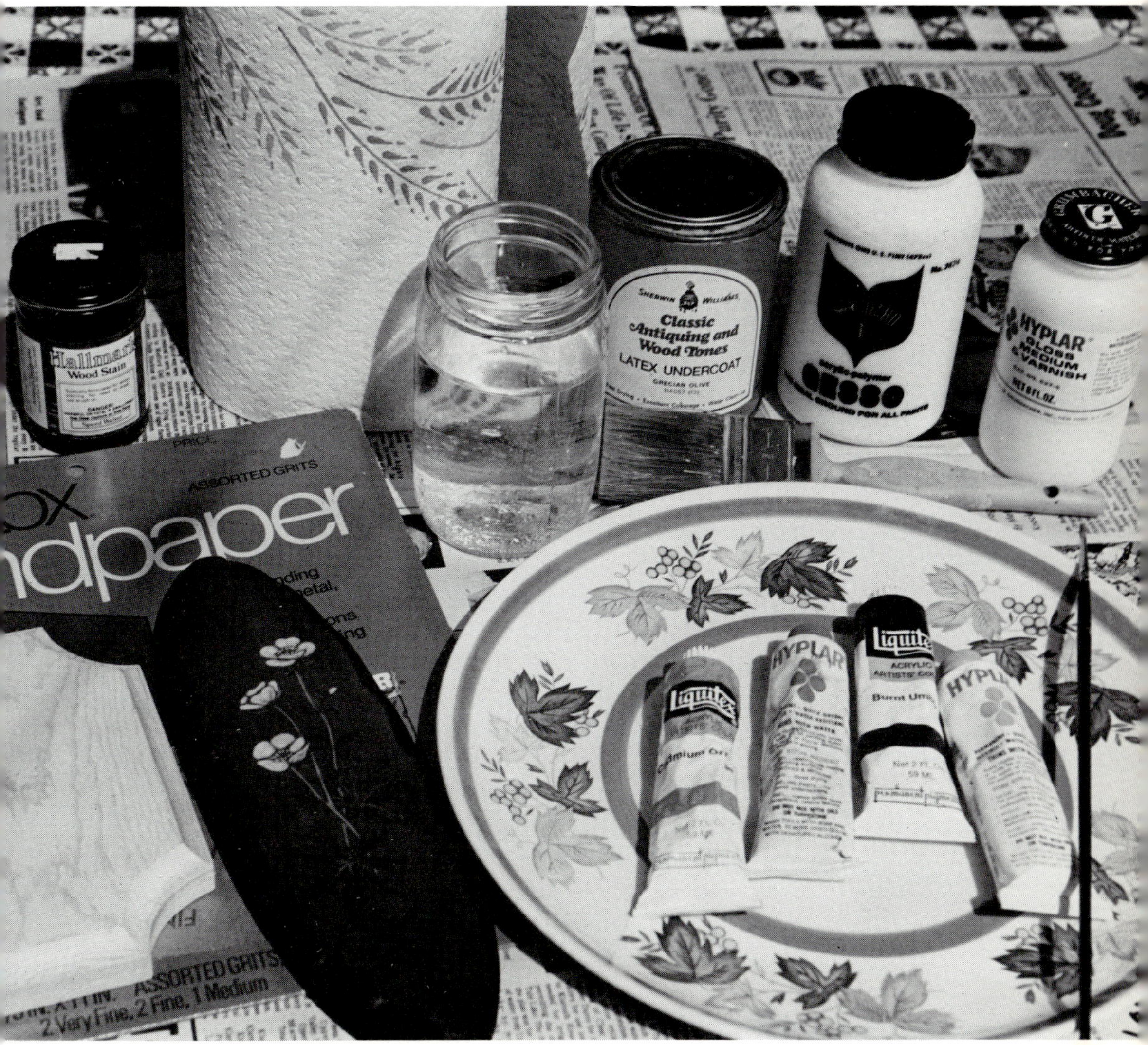

Few materials are required for painting the crafts in this book: some basic acrylic colors, brushes, gloss polymer medium, and an old plate for a palette.

Other materials needed are:

- Gesso
- Gloss polymer medium (a white liquid that dries to a glossy finish)
- Wood stain
- Umber antiquing stain
- Sandpaper
- Paper towels
- Latex paint for painting base color on large objects

3
Painting with Acrylics

An old porcelain plate serves well as a paint palette. Have paper towels handy for cleaning brushes and for wipe-ups. You will need a jar of water. Always wet your brush before dipping it in paint. Since acrylic paint is quick drying, place the brushes in water immediately after using to prevent the paint from hardening on the bristles. Wear an old smock; acrylics are permanent!

To avoid smearing of the traced design, stain or paint the base coat on the object first, allow to dry, then trace on the design. Use carbon paper on light backgrounds. Chalk rubbed on the back of the design is a good way to trace on dark-stained objects. Go over the traced lines with a thin line of umber or black before proceeding with the painting.

Shade as you paint by following this method: work from dark to light. Thin the first application with water. (The paint should be of a creamy consistency.) Next, using this undercoat as a shaded area, paint over with the same color, but undiluted with water, highlighting where desirable. You will notice that the second coat is more brilliant. Do not attempt to paint too thickly. Keep it smooth. For stronger highlights, add a bit of white or yellow to the color.

Remember to keep the light direction from one source: right or left. Be consistent in this throughout your design.

On a slickly varnished surface, the paint thinned with water may tend to bead and not stick evenly. If this happens, use the acrylics full strength without diluting.

Keep in mind the basic color-mixing formula:

red + yellow makes orange
yellow + blue makes green
blue + red makes violet

Add white to tint lighter; black to shade darker.

4
Painting on Wood

Wood is a delightful surface on which to use acrylic paint. Ready-made, undecorated wood items are to be found everywhere: in your home, at garage sales and flea markets, in variety stores and craft shops. They may be unfinished or already stained and ready to design. Be sure they are sanded smooth. If an item is highly varnished, it may be necessary to dull it with a light rubbing with steel wool so that the acrylic paint goes on smoothly.

If you are handy with a saw (or know someone who is), you may enjoy constructing your own wood items for painting.

Acrylic paint dries to a soft mat finish and needs no further varnish. However, if a glossy appearance is preferred, or if the craft to be used must withstand extra wear, it may be finished with a coat of gloss polymer medium.

CHIPMUNK AND COLUMBINE

Stain the unfinished wood barrel with walnut stain. Allow to dry overnight. Brush on a thin mixture of yellow ocher and water for the background color of the design. Trace the design using carbon, or if the background is too dark, rub chalk on the back of the pattern to transfer.

Paint grasses first: some yellow ocher, some green by mixing thalo blue and cadmium yellow light.

Columbine: cadmium red light and cadmium yellow medium.

Chipmunk: to shade the white areas, thin the white paint with water for the first coat; it will be grayed. Now highlight with undiluted white. Yellow ocher, burnt sienna, and black are used for the body.

With a small brush, outline the design with black for further emphasis. You may do this after tracing the pattern to keep the lines from smearing, then go over the outline again after the design is painted.

The barrel needs no further finish, but if a gloss is desired, give it a coat of gloss polymer medium.

Wooden Barrel with Chipmunk and Columbine

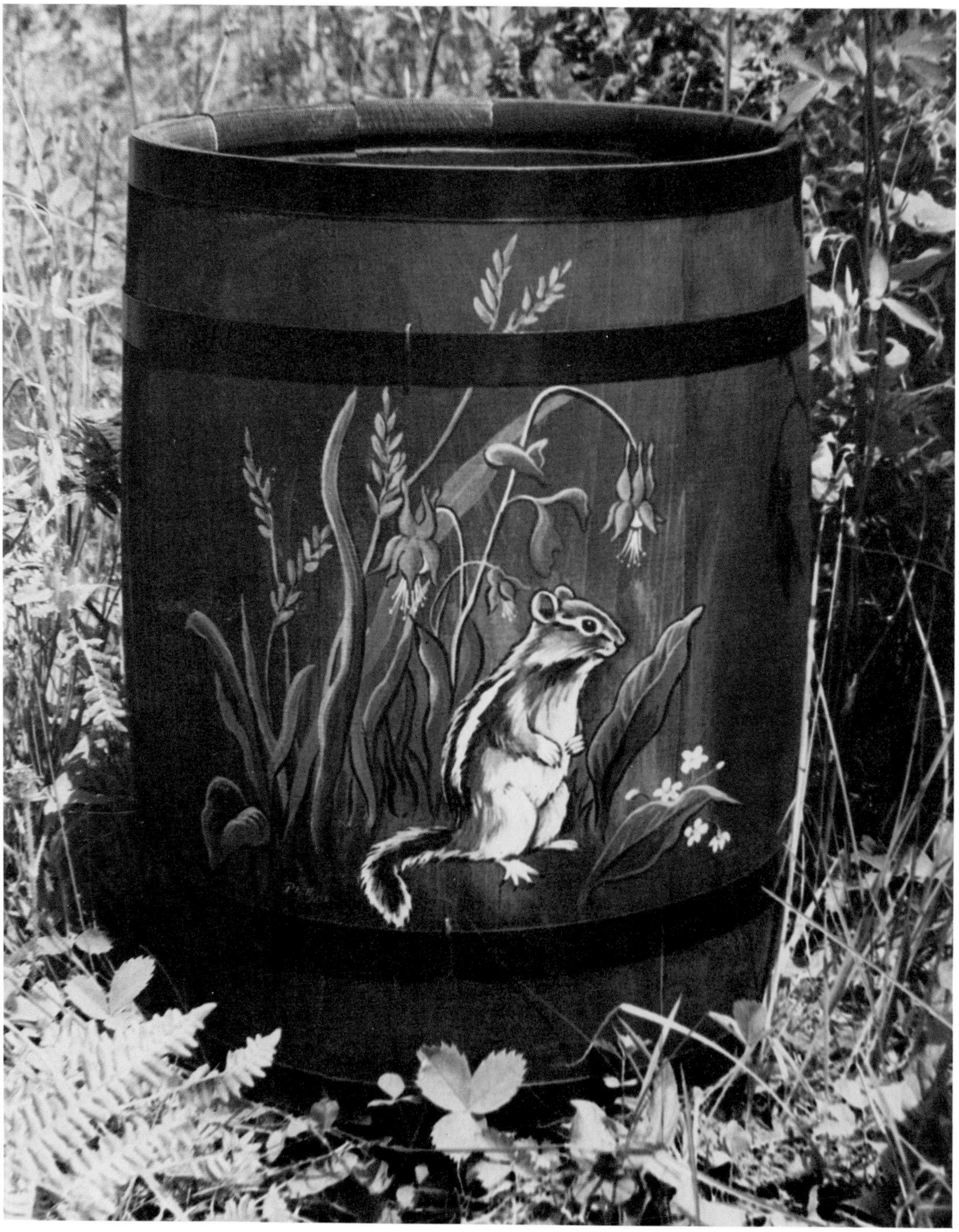

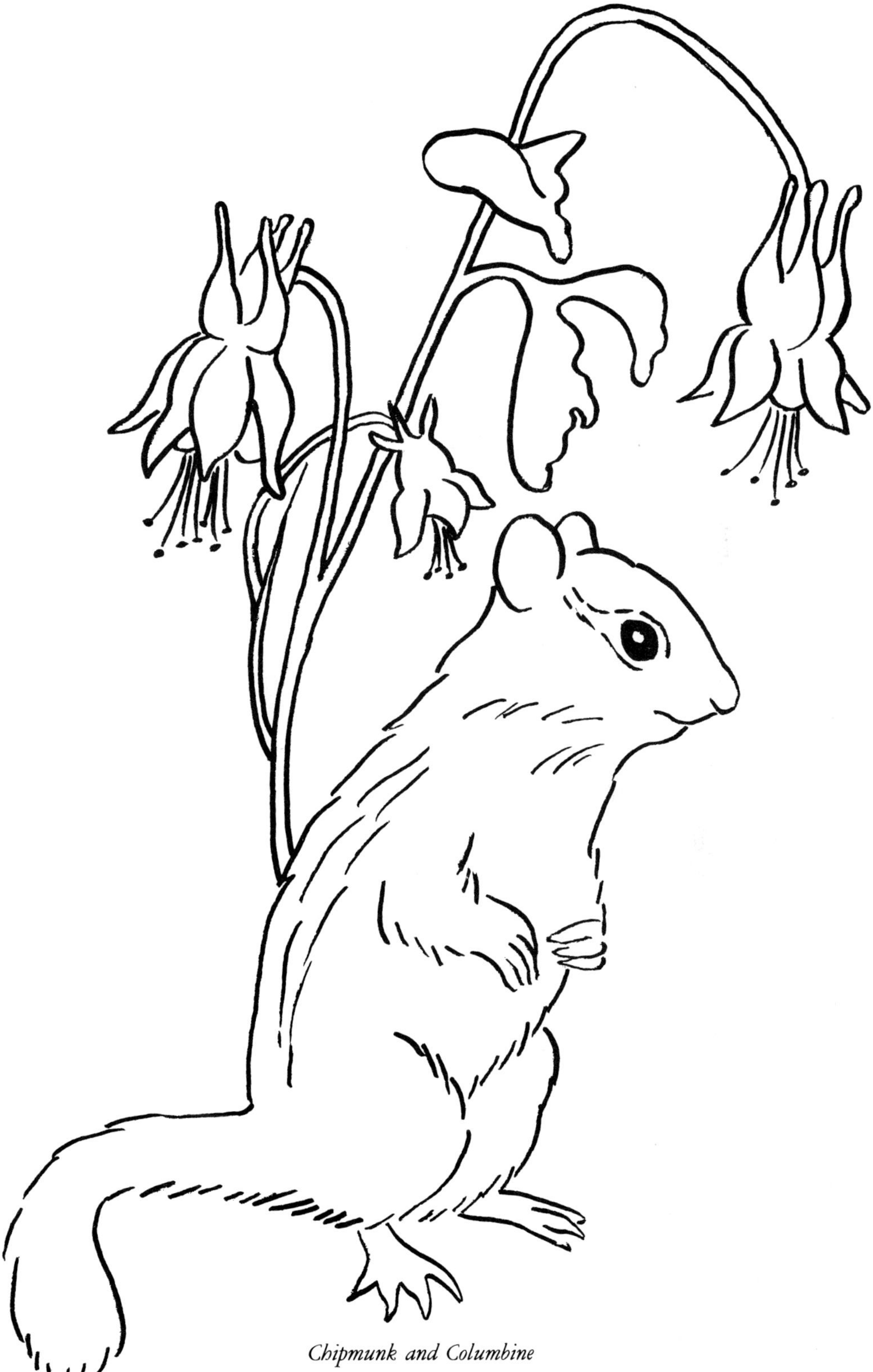

Chipmunk and Columbine

CALIFORNIA POPPIES

Sand the unfinished wood dish and give it a base coat of thalo green. The border and the back of the dish are a lighter green, made by mixing cadmium yellow with a small amount of thalo green. Trace on the design.

Poppies are three shades: cadmium yellow medium, orange, and the centers are cadmium yellow mixed with burnt sienna. The leaves and stems are the same shade of yellow green as the border.

Finish with a varnish of gloss polymer medium.

Wooden Dish with California Poppies

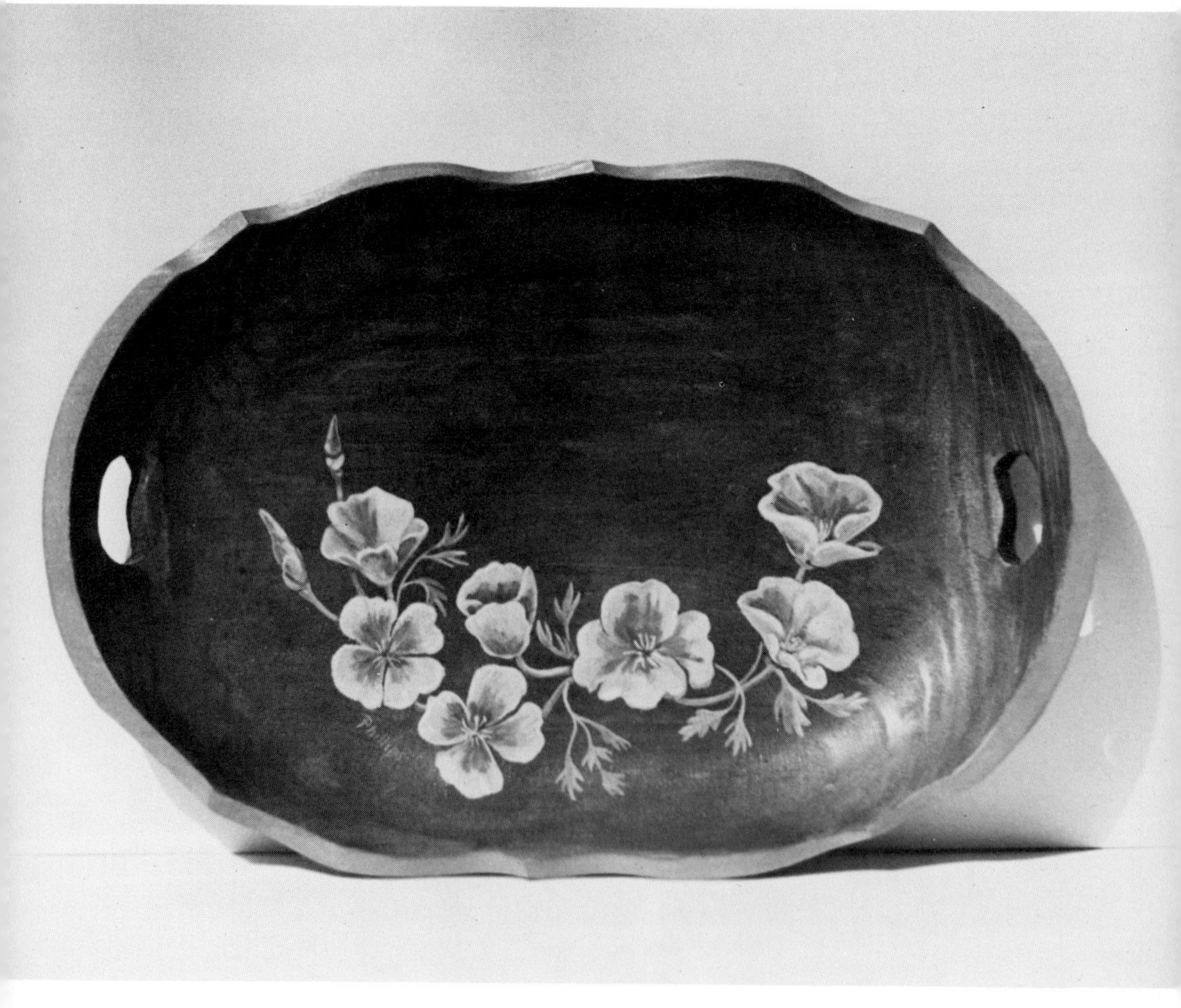

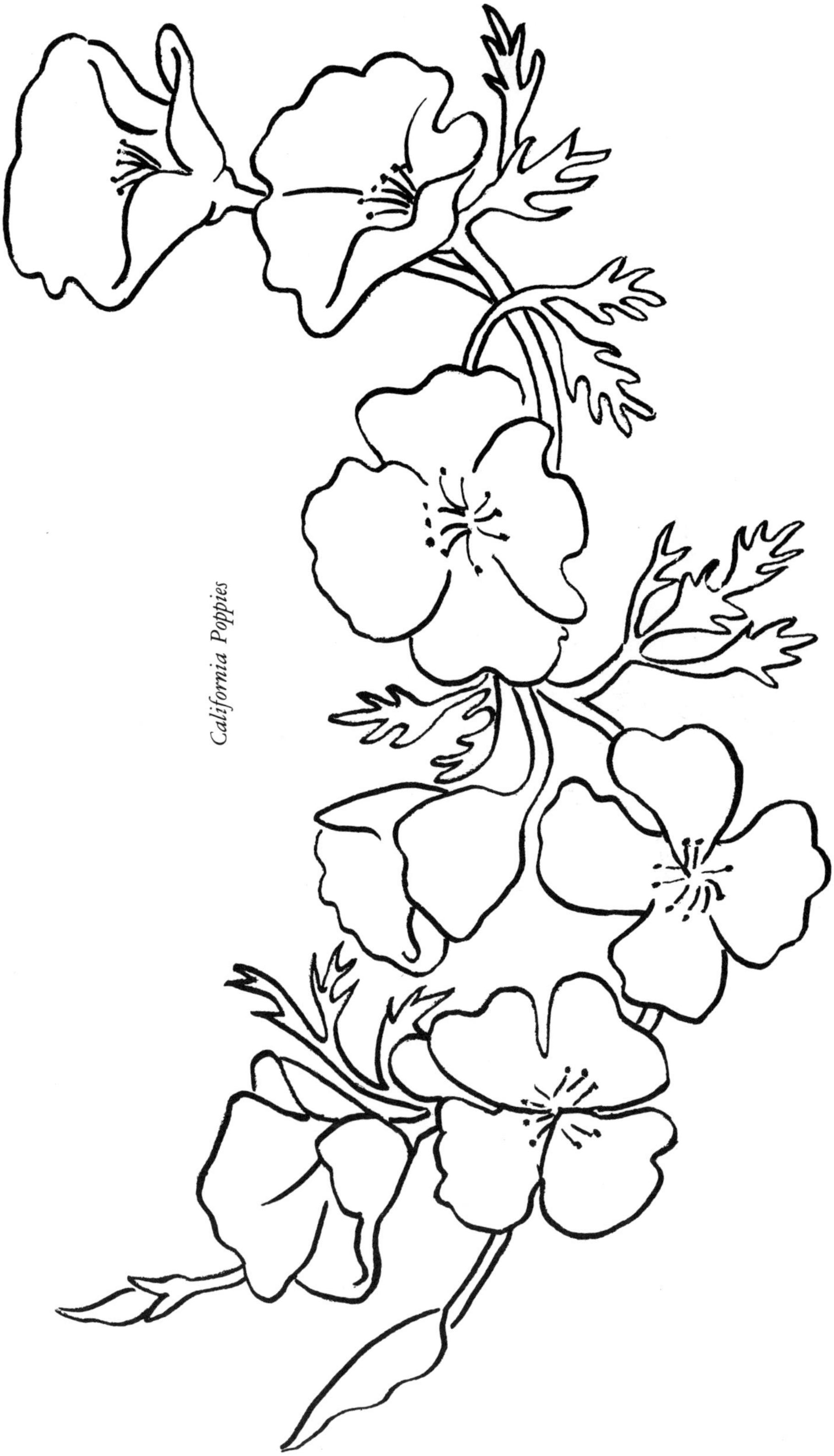

California Poppies

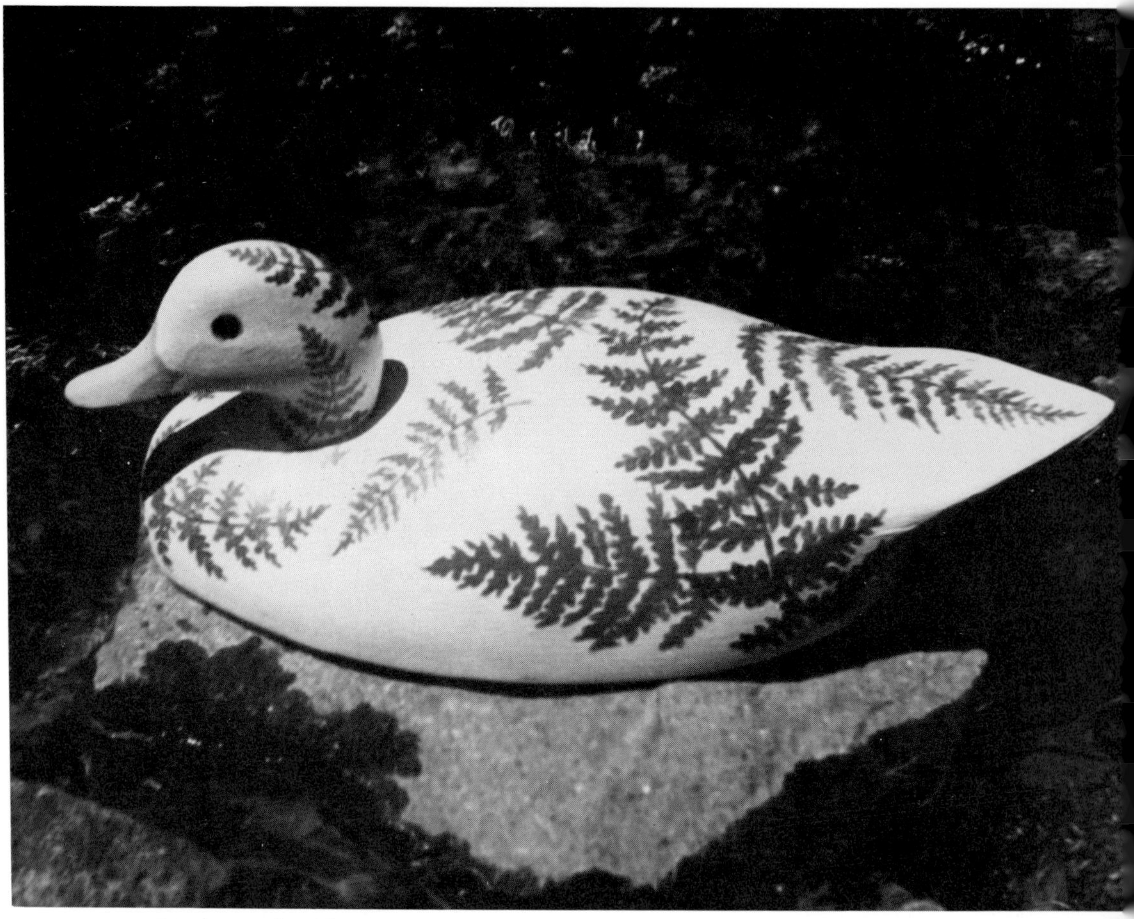

Wooden Duck with Ferns

FERNS

The wooden duck was purchased in a store that sells unfinished furniture. It could, of course, have been painted in natural colors with acrylic. I chose a whimsical pattern of ferns instead. Flowers would have worked equally as well.

Sand the unfinished wood duck smoothly, and give it a base coat of gesso. When thoroughly dry, give it a second coat of white paint.

The ferns are two shades of green: thalo blue mixed with cadmium yellow and thalo blue mixed with yellow ocher. The duck's bill is cadmium yellow. Finish with a glaze of gloss polymer medium.

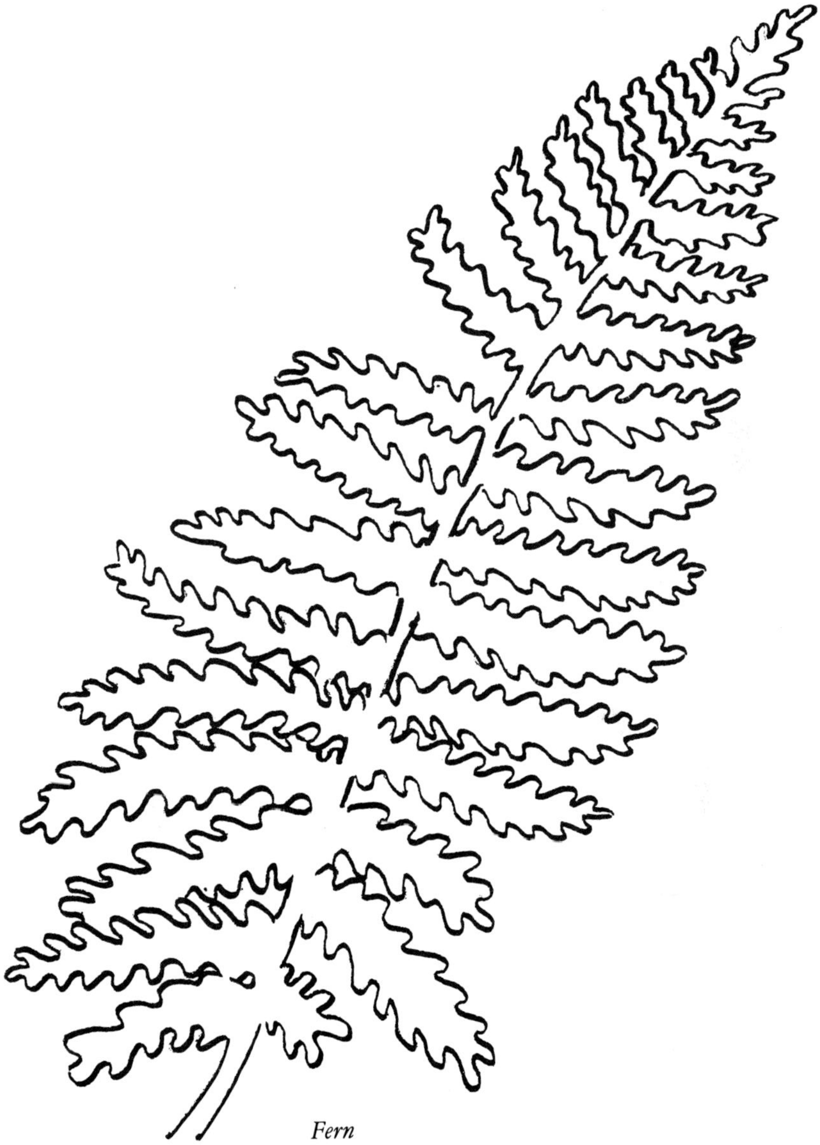

Fern

RABBITS AND DANDELIONS

The towel holder was originally stained a darker color. It is sanded and given a new base coat of olive green. Since it is quite large, a latex paint is used to cover the entire holder. The moon is painted with one coat of white. Next the rest of the design is traced on and outlined with burnt umber.

The dandelions are cadmium yellow and orange; the leaves are thalo green and cadmium yellow.

The rabbits are white, burnt umber, and black.

After the design is painted, it is antiqued with a commercial antiquing glaze of umber, following the directions on the label. It is painted over the entire surface and, after a few minutes, wiped off with a soft cloth, leaving the glaze in cracks and corners. No additional finish is needed.

Towel Holder with Rabbits and Dandelions

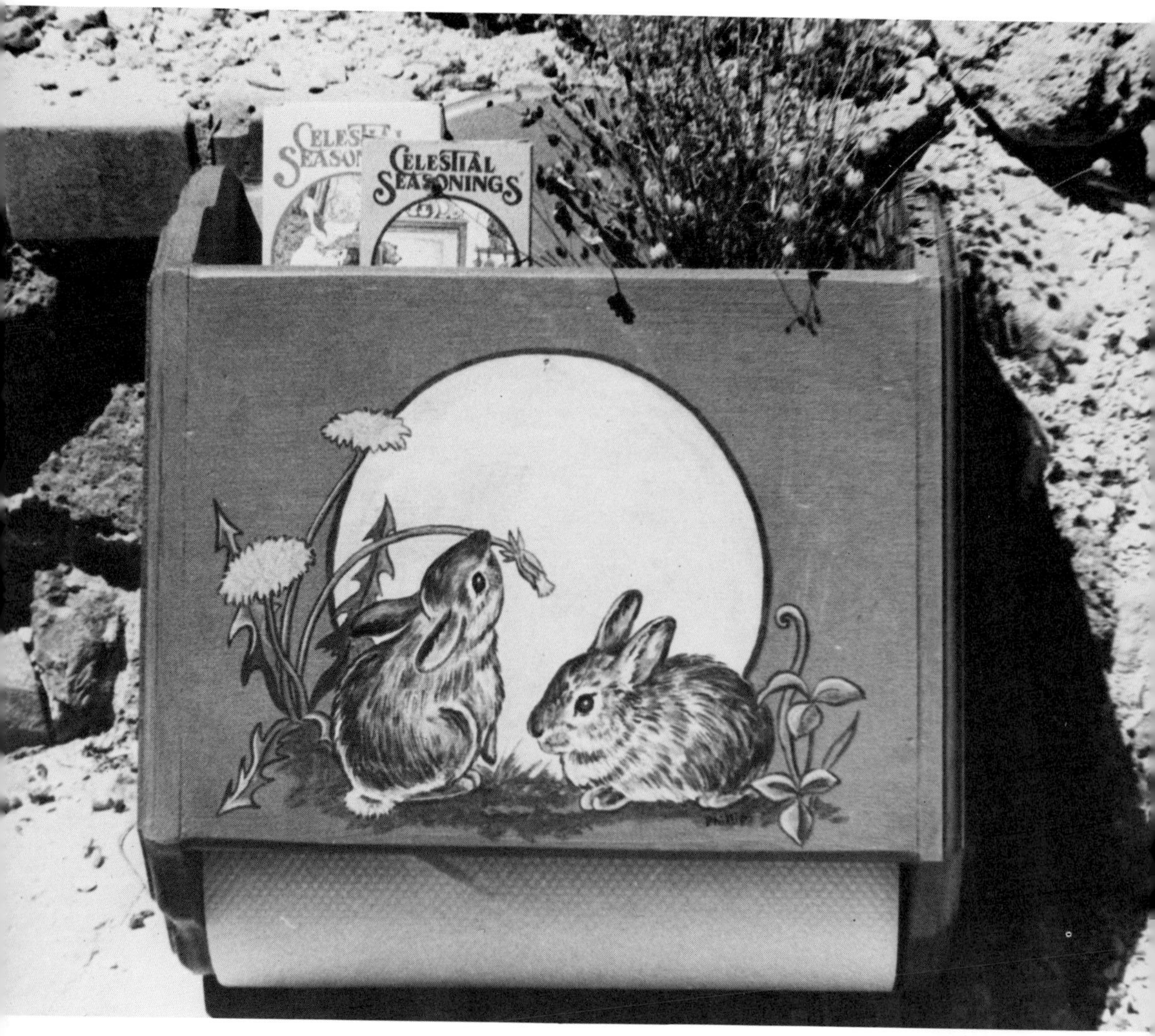

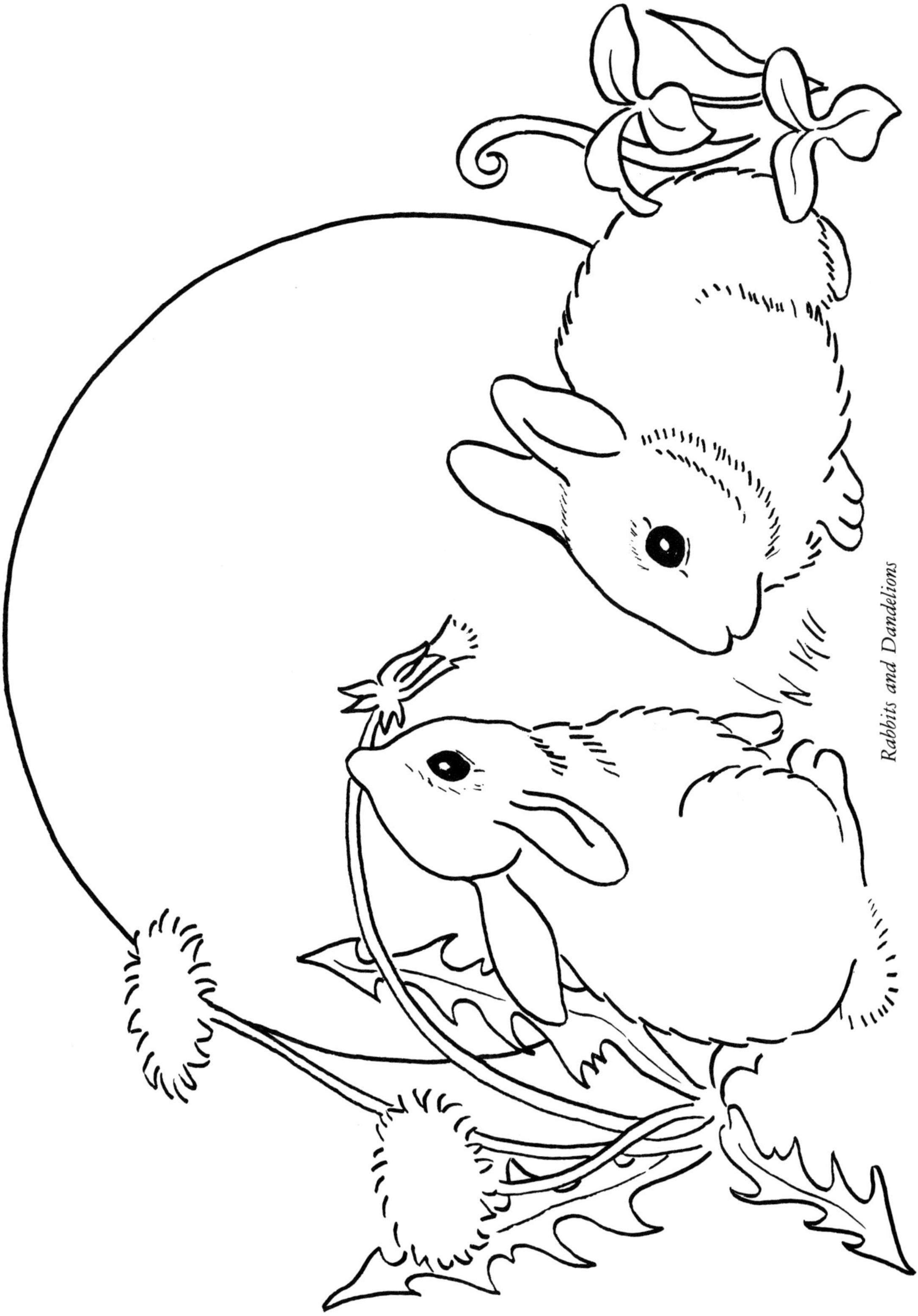

Rabbits and Dandelions

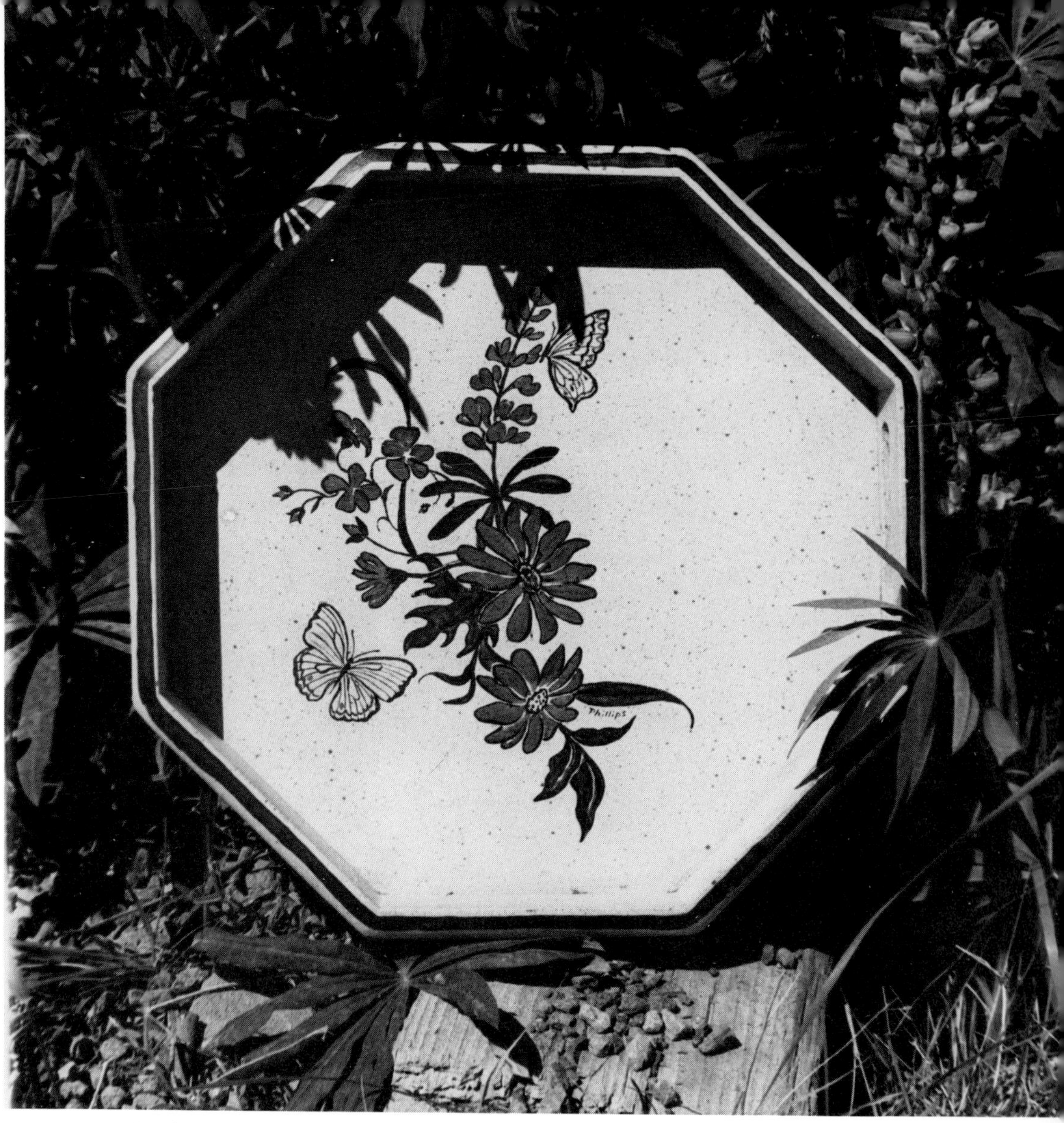

Serving Tray with Lupine and Daisies

LUPINE AND DAISIES

The unfinished wood serving tray is given a base coat and antiqued *before* the design is added.

Directions are as follows: Sand the tray and give it two coats of white, allowing it to dry thoroughly between coats. When dry, paint it with an umber antiquing glaze, wait a few minutes, and wipe away the glaze by stroking with a soft cloth in one direction. A spatter effect may be achieved by dipping a small stiff brush (an old toothbrush will do) into the glaze and rubbing the thumb across the brush causing a spray of tiny drops. Cover the working area with plenty of old papers before starting this project. Allow to dry overnight.

The stylized design is painted using just two colors: thalo blue for all the flowers and burnt umber for the leaves and stems. Outline the blue flowers with a thin line of burnt umber.

For extra durability, finish with two coats of gloss polymer medium.

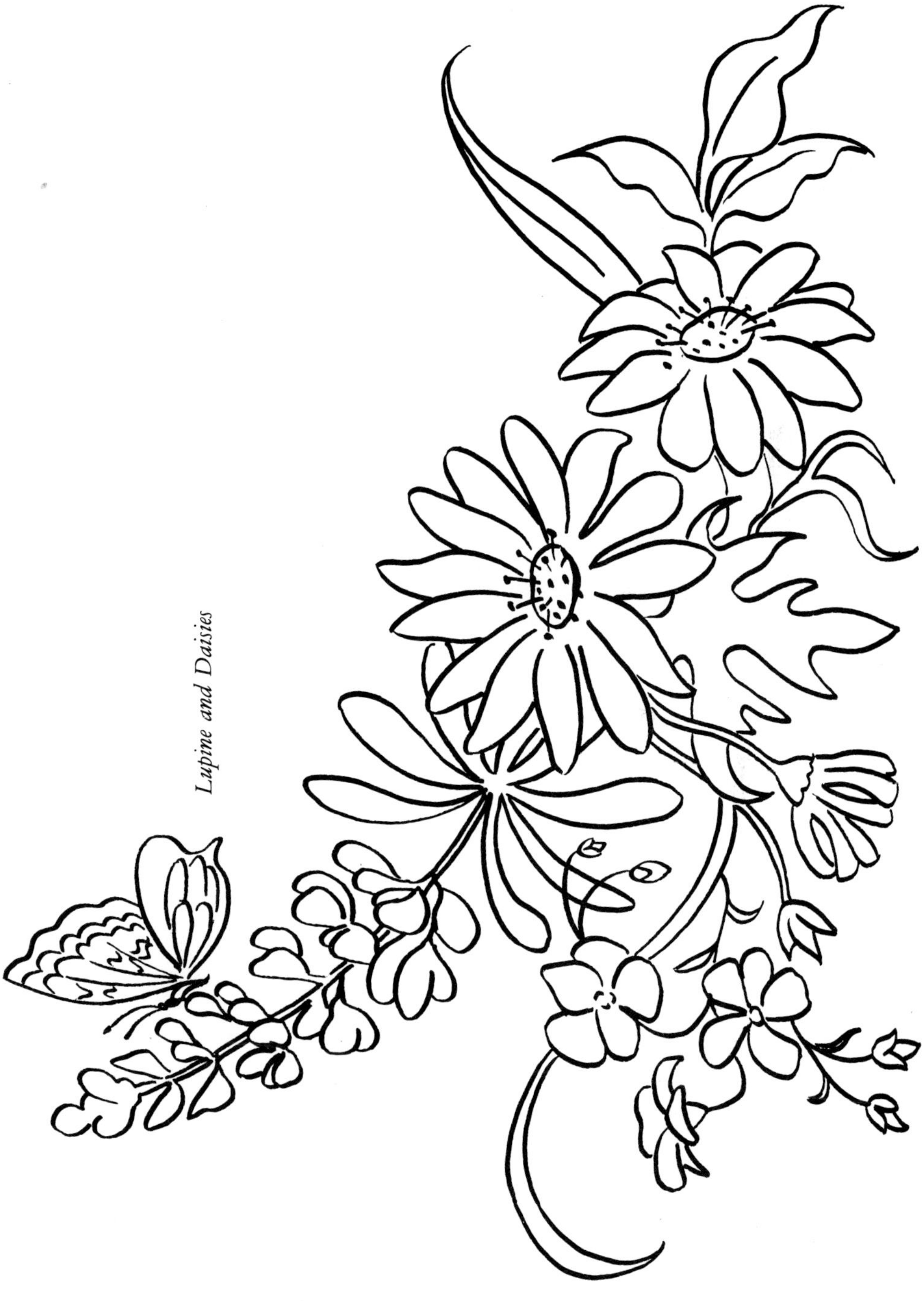

Lupine and Daisies

WILD ROSES

An old music box is given a new design of wild roses. To paint a similar one, give the box two coats of off-white: titanium white tinted with a small amount of umber. The paint should be the consistency of thick cream. Trace the design.

The wild roses are pink: a small amount of Naphthol crimson red mixed with white. The leaves are thalo blue, cadmium yellow, and a touch of white to make a pale green. Outline with umber to emphasize the design.

If desired, the box may be trimmed with acrylic metallic gold.

Finish with gloss polymer medium.

Music Box with Wild Roses

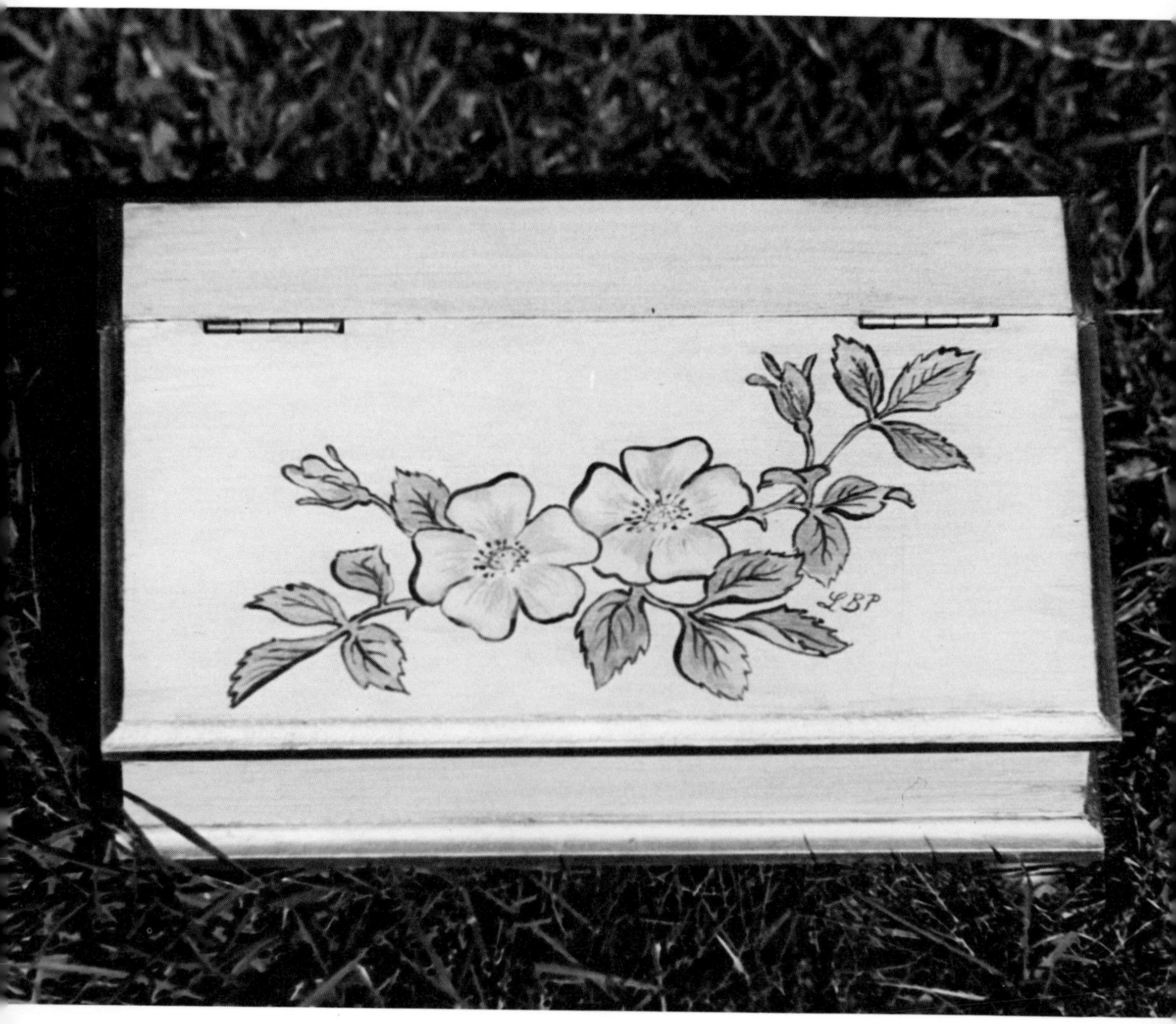

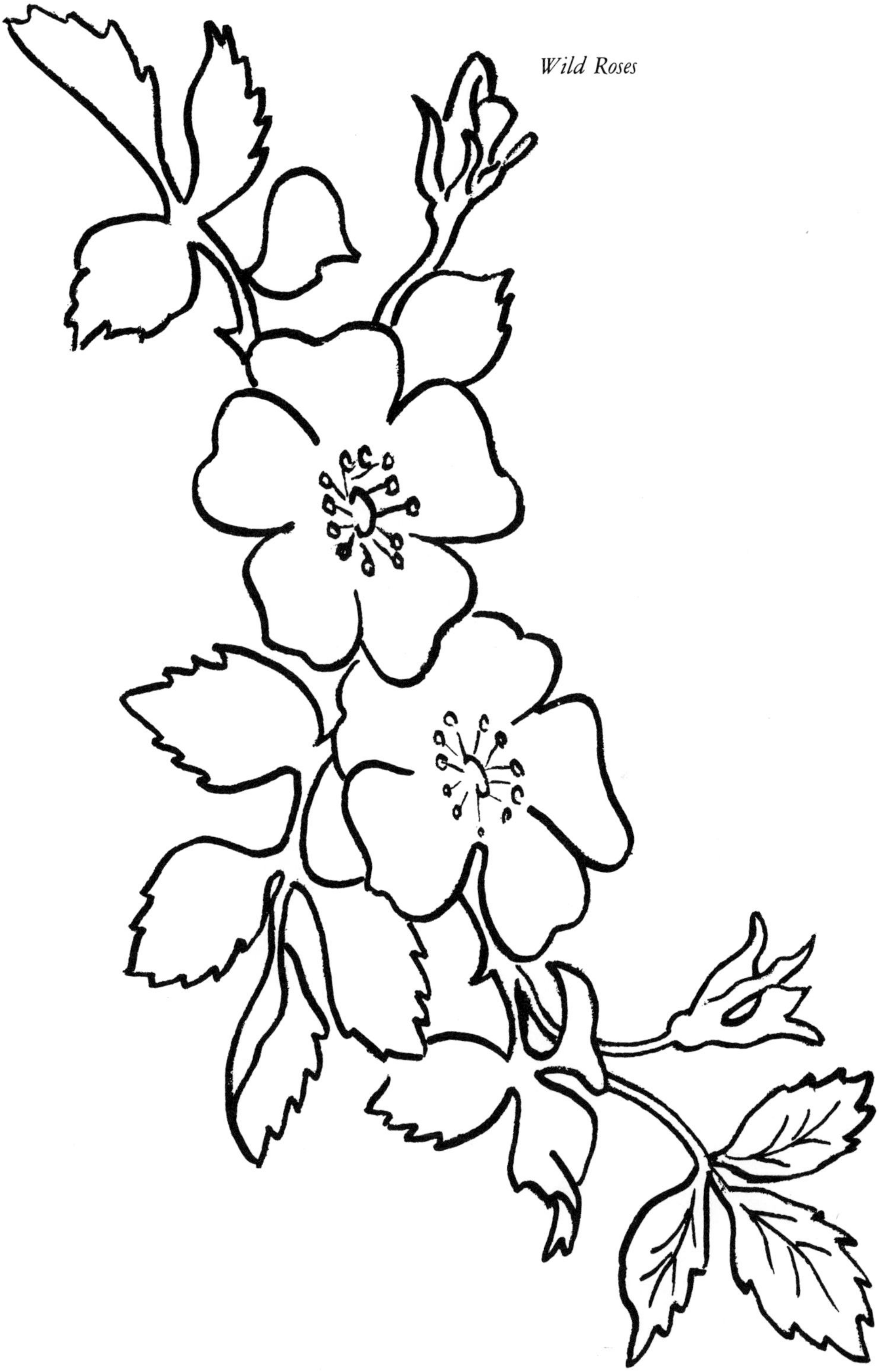

Wild Roses

QUEEN ANNE'S LACE

These will be the simplest flowers you have ever painted! The flowers are nothing more than a mass of dots. The design is applied to a lap desk box, but you may use any kind of wood box.

Paint the unfinished box inside and out with a base coat. An olive green latex is used here. Trace the design with carbon paper. The dark green foliage is painted with a mixture of thalo blue and cadmium yellow. Add a little white for highlights. Use a small pointed brush and dab on water-thinned white paint. The first coat is the shading. Next, go over the flowers with undiluted white to add highlights.

Lap Desk with Queen Anne's Lace

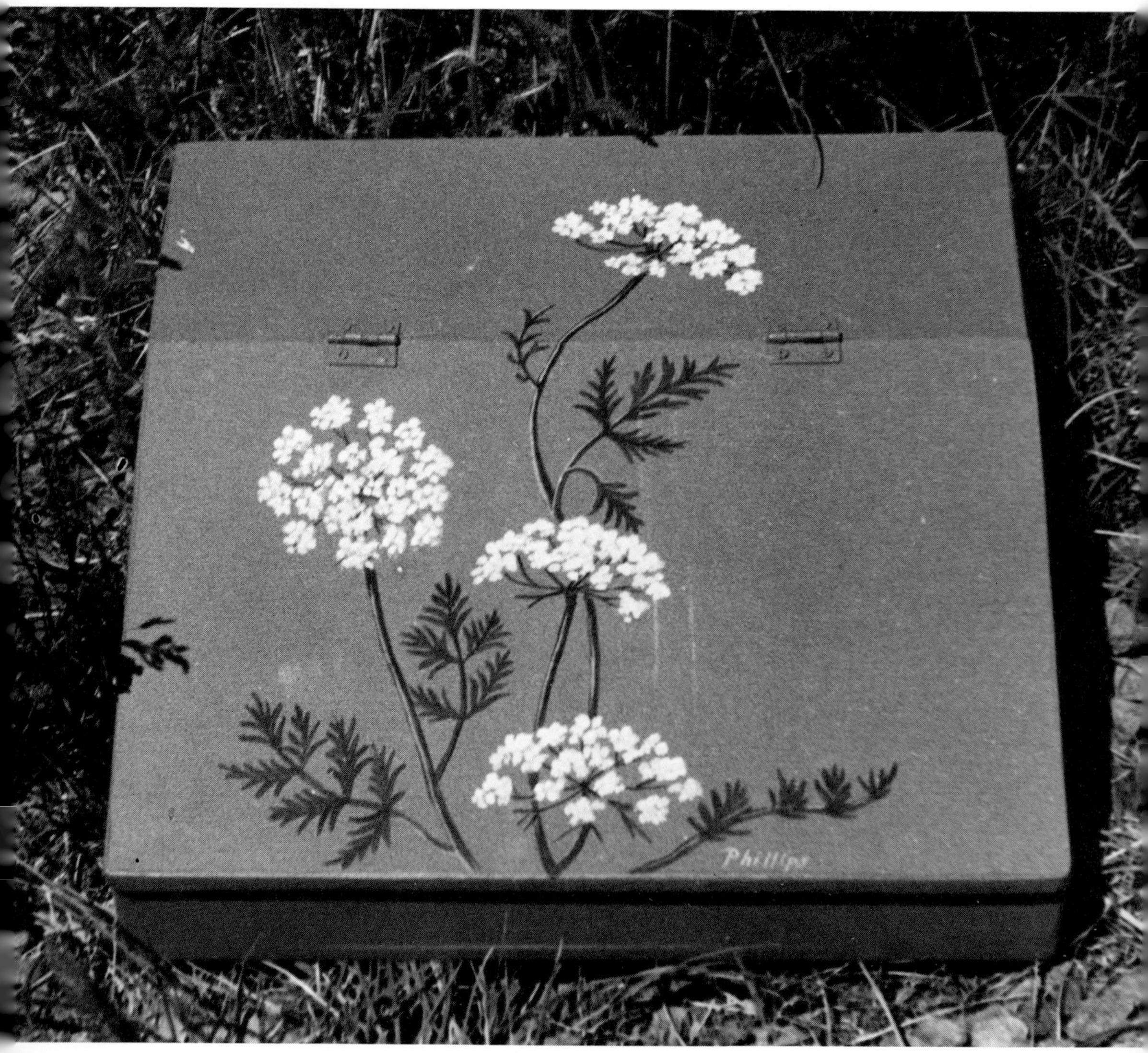

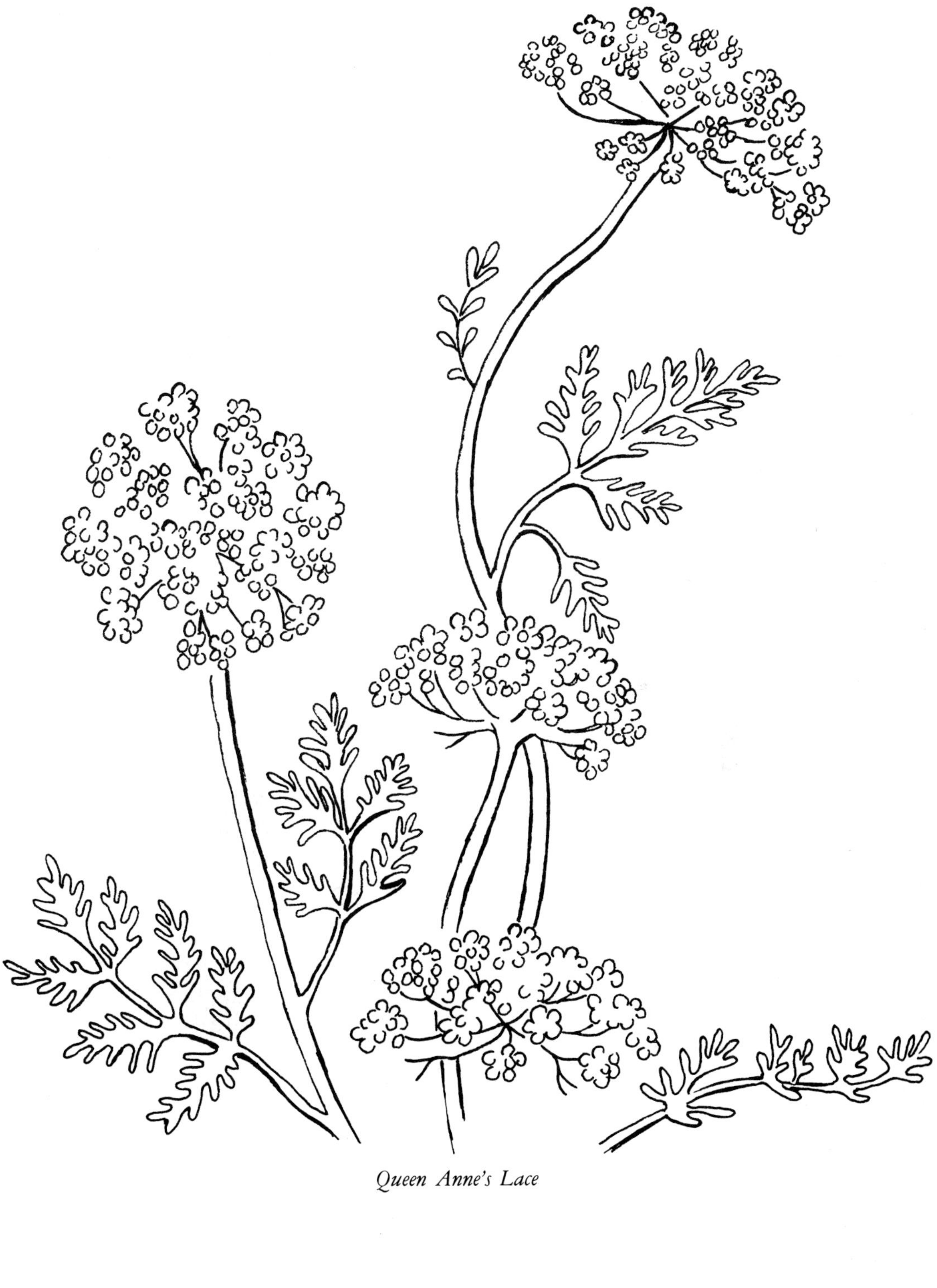

Queen Anne's Lace

WILD STRAWBERRIES AND FLOWER BOUQUET

The bucket planter and kitchen utensils were purchased already stained. They just lacked a personal touch of a design in acrylic. Once you begin looking for paintables, you will find lots of things in your own kitchen that will be enhanced by the addition of a handpainted design.

Paint the strawberries with cadmium red and a touch of white; the leaves are thalo blue and cadmium yellow.

For the kitchen utensils, choose flower patterns of a form best suited to the shape of the utensils. Paint the stems right down to the handles, and you have a bouquet of wild flowers!

Wild Strawberries on Bucket Planter

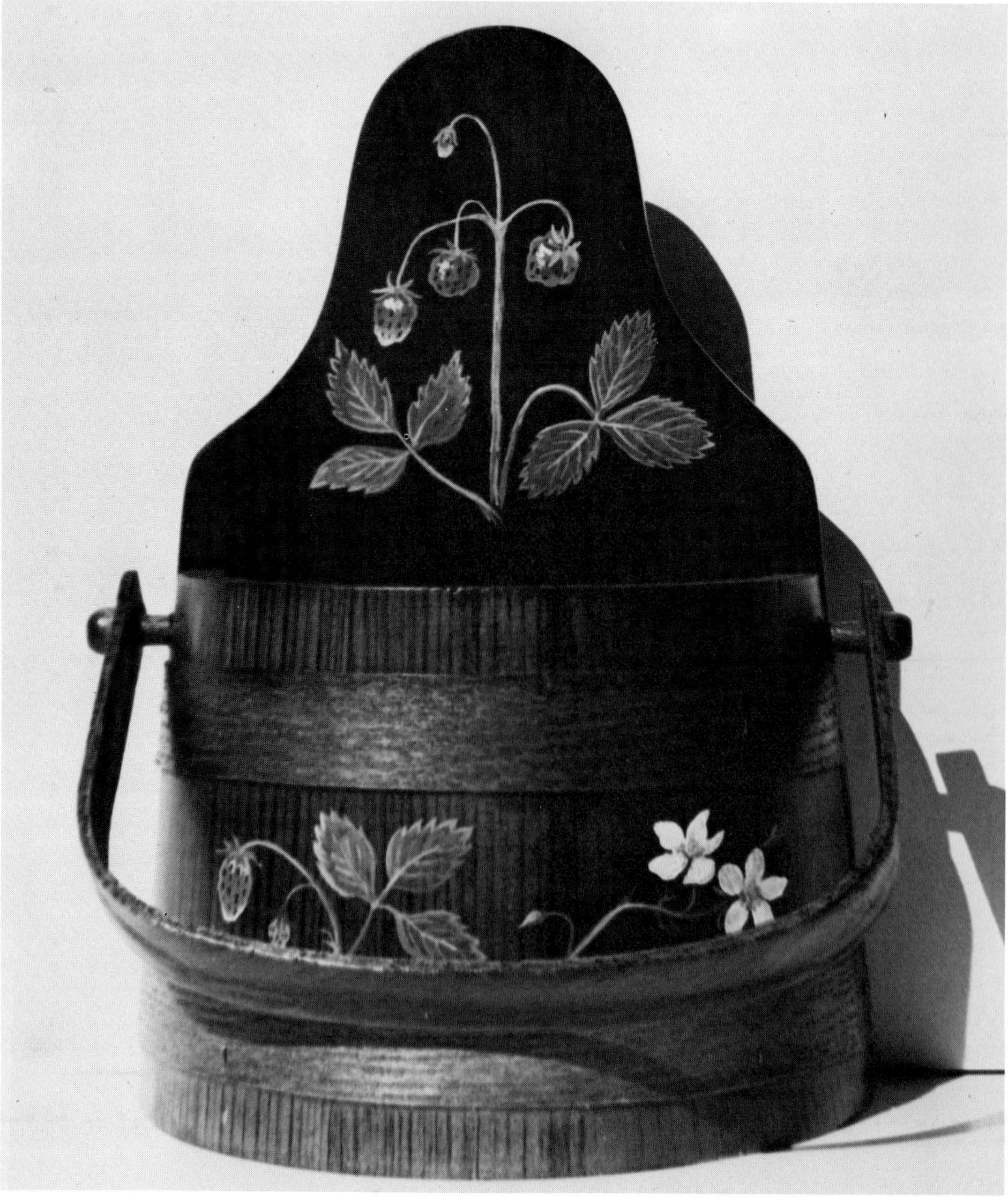

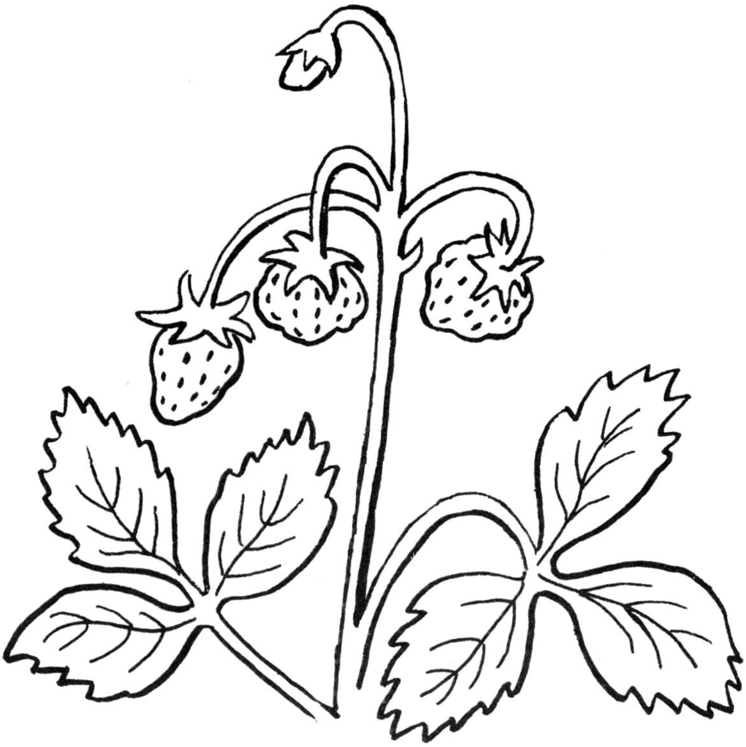

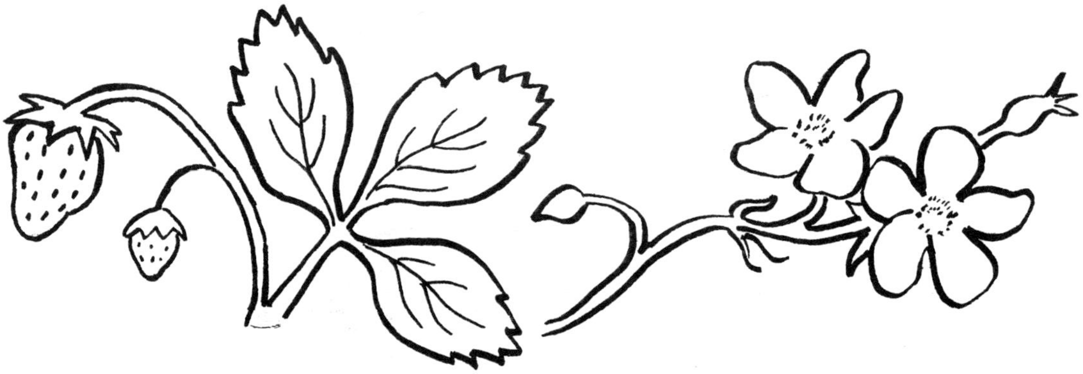

Wild Strawberries

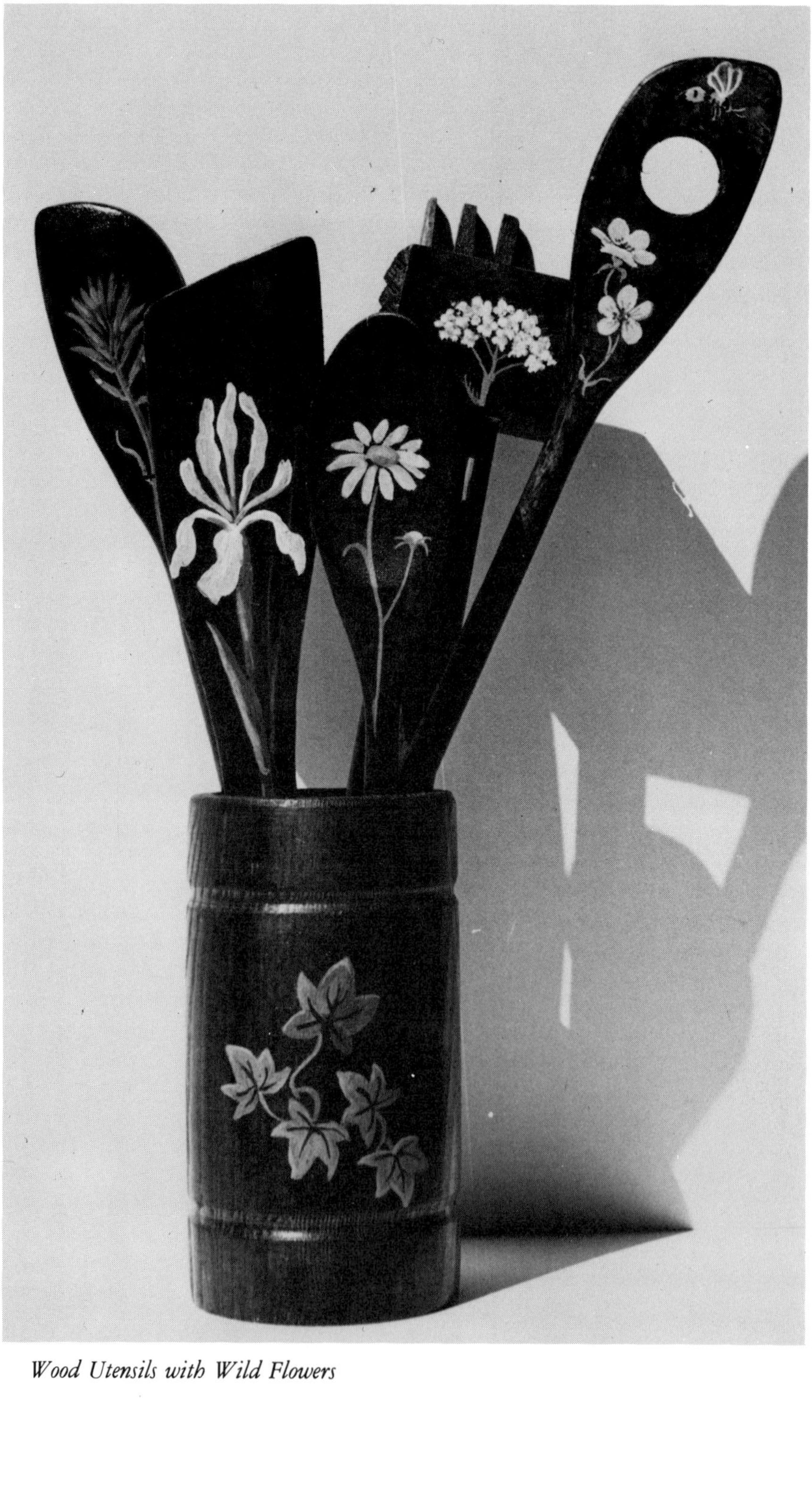

Wood Utensils with Wild Flowers

Painting on Wood Plaques

Wood plaques can be made from scraps of lumber or from purchased precut forms. Sand the wood smooth and it is ready to design, either stained or unstained.

BUTTERCUPS

The buttercups are painted on the natural wood, only the edge is stained umber. The colors used: cadmium yellow, the petals are outlined with yellow ocher; the green of the leaves and stems is a mixture of cadmium yellow and thalo blue.

It is varnished with one coat of polymer medium.

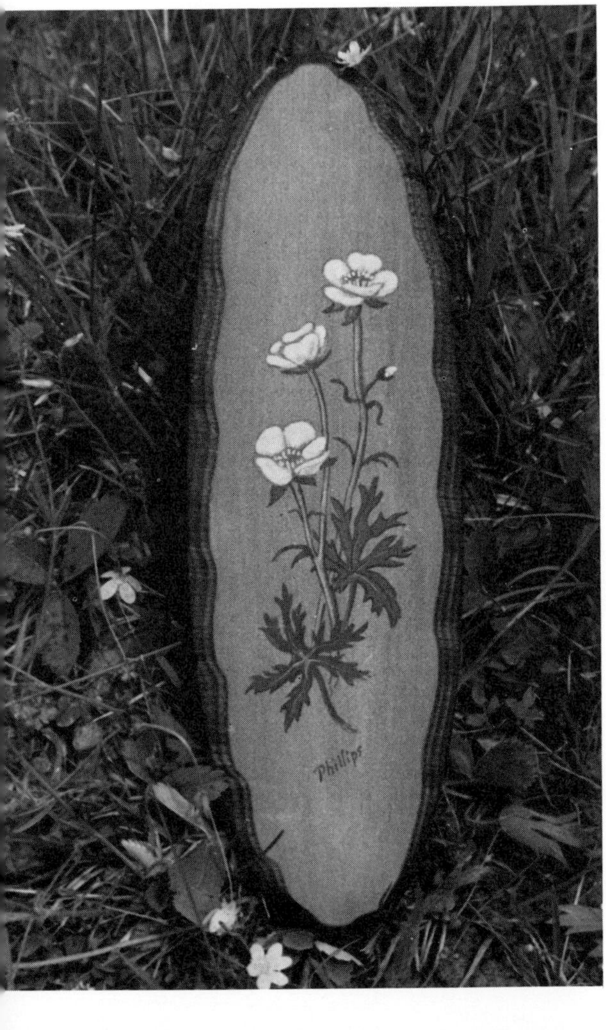

Buttercup Plaque

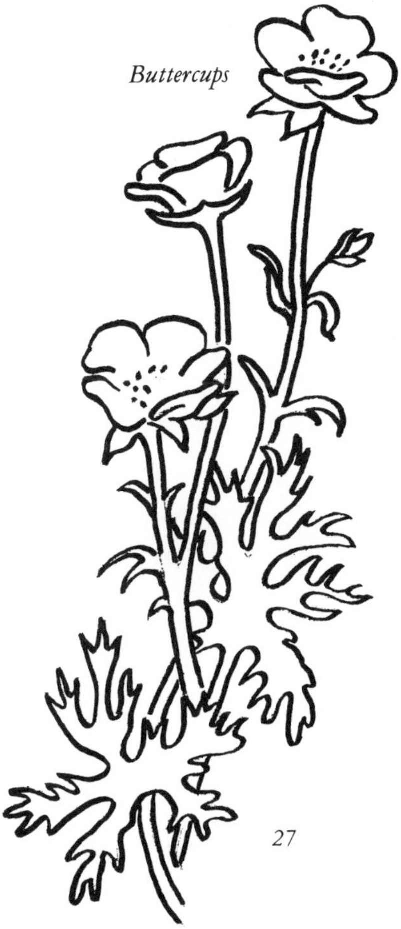

Buttercups

RACCOONS

Lightly stain the plaque board with a thin mixture of burnt umber. Brush yellow ocher thinned with water on the background; this may be quickly rubbed on with a small wad of paper towel. When dry, trace on the design with carbon paper. With a small brush, go over all the lines of the tracing with burnt umber. Paint the design using the following colors: raccoons, black, burnt umber, and white; fence, white and burnt umber; grasses, green made with thalo blue and cadmium yellow.

Raccoon Plaque

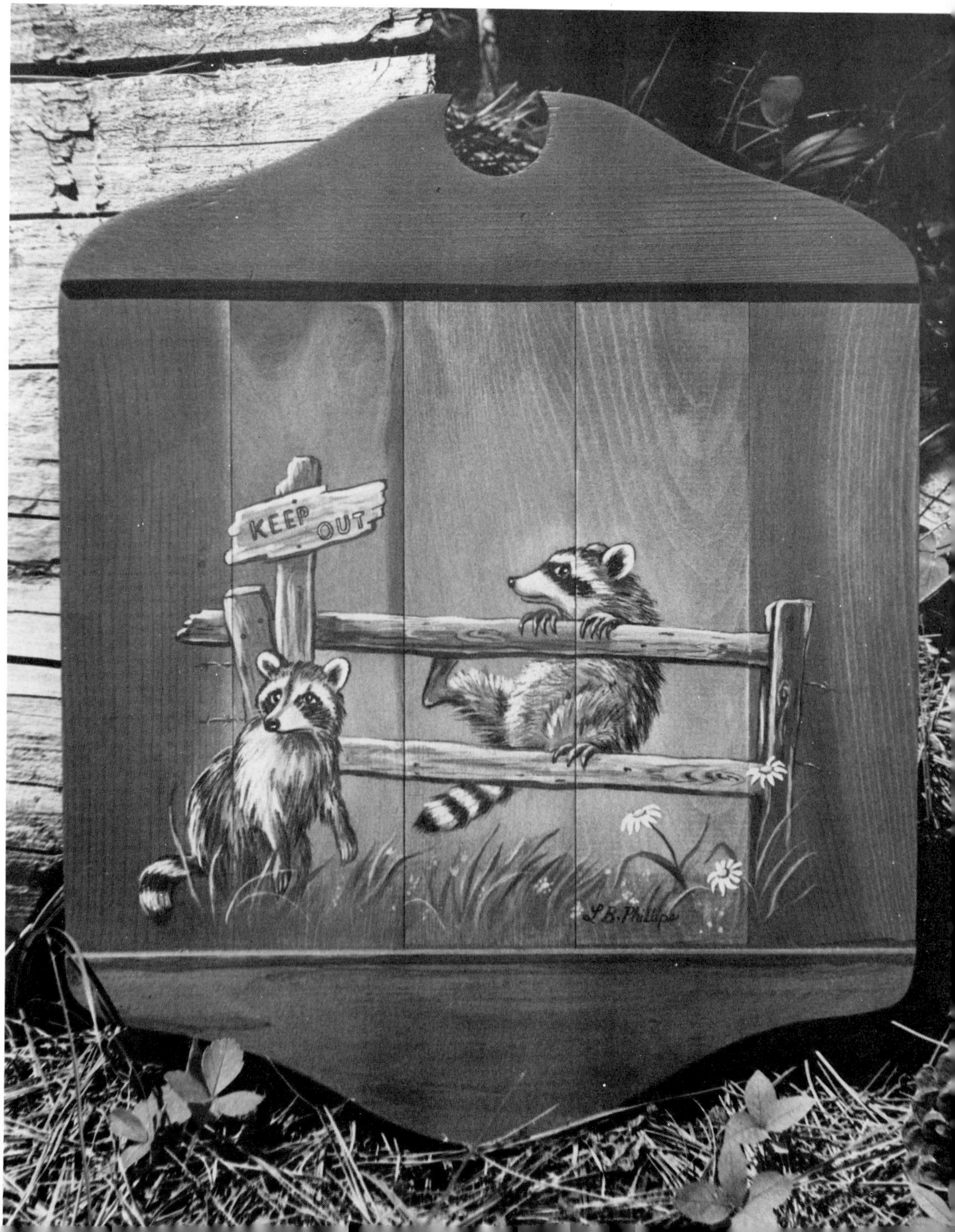

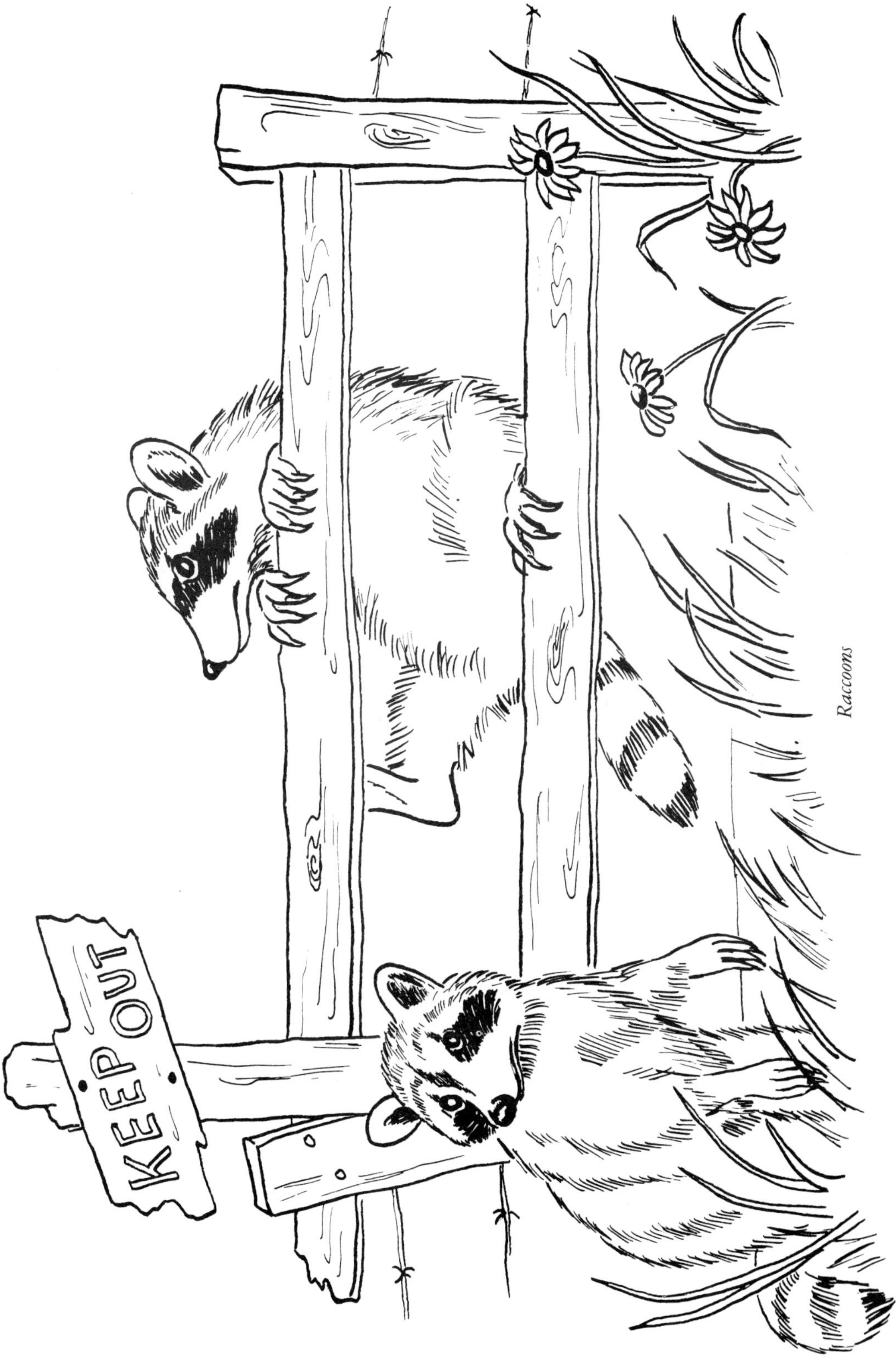

Raccoons

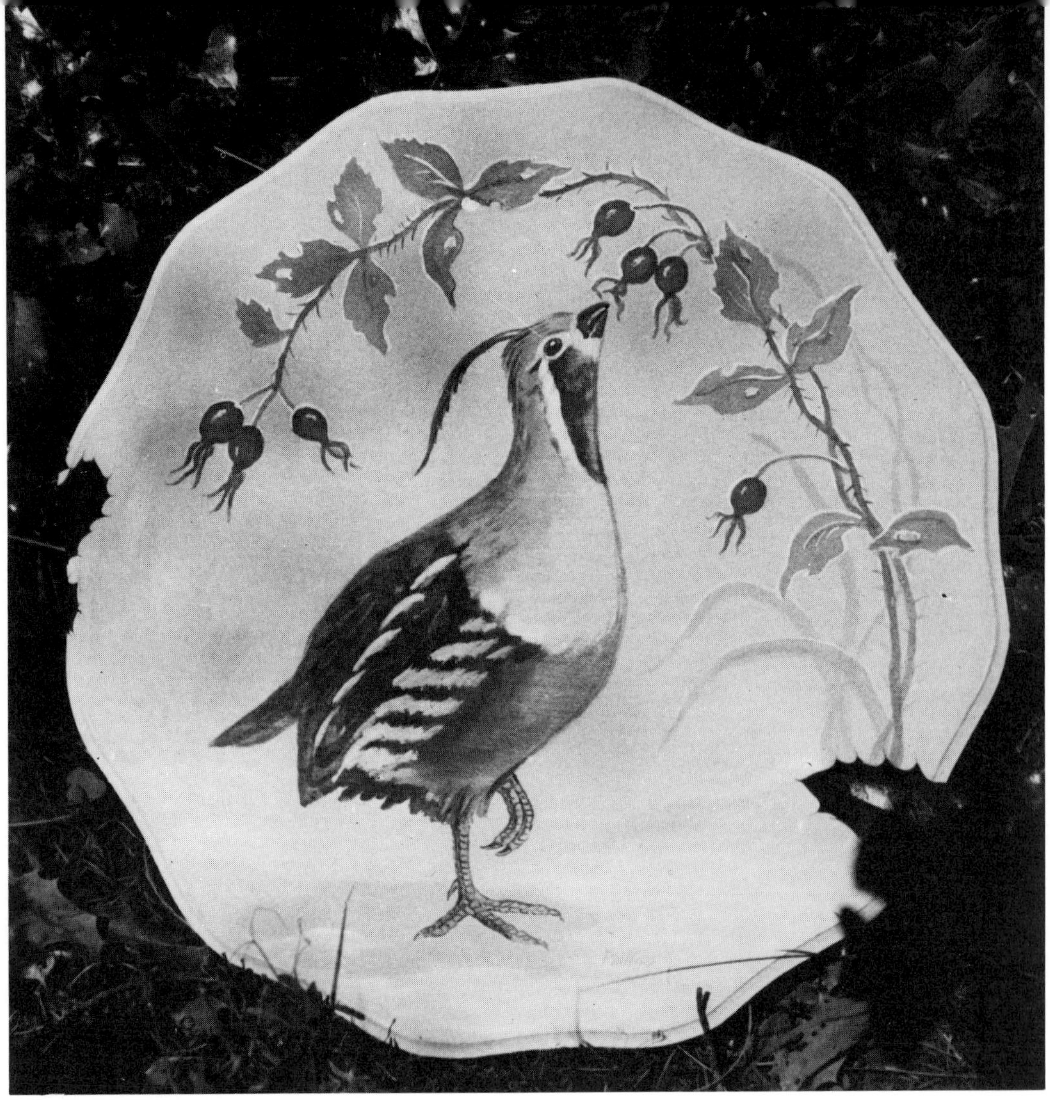

Mountain Quail and Rose Hip Plaque

MOUNTAIN QUAIL AND ROSE HIPS

Paint the board a base coat of white using gesso or titanium white. Background color; a thin mixture of white and thalo blue can be effectively applied by using a wad of paper towel. This method helps blend the paint smoothly onto the wood. Add white for snow near the bottom of the plaque.

Colors of the quail: gray mixed from black and white; quail's back, burnt umber; breast, burnt sienna.

Rose hips are cadmium red; leaves are yellow ocher. The foliage is outlined with white.

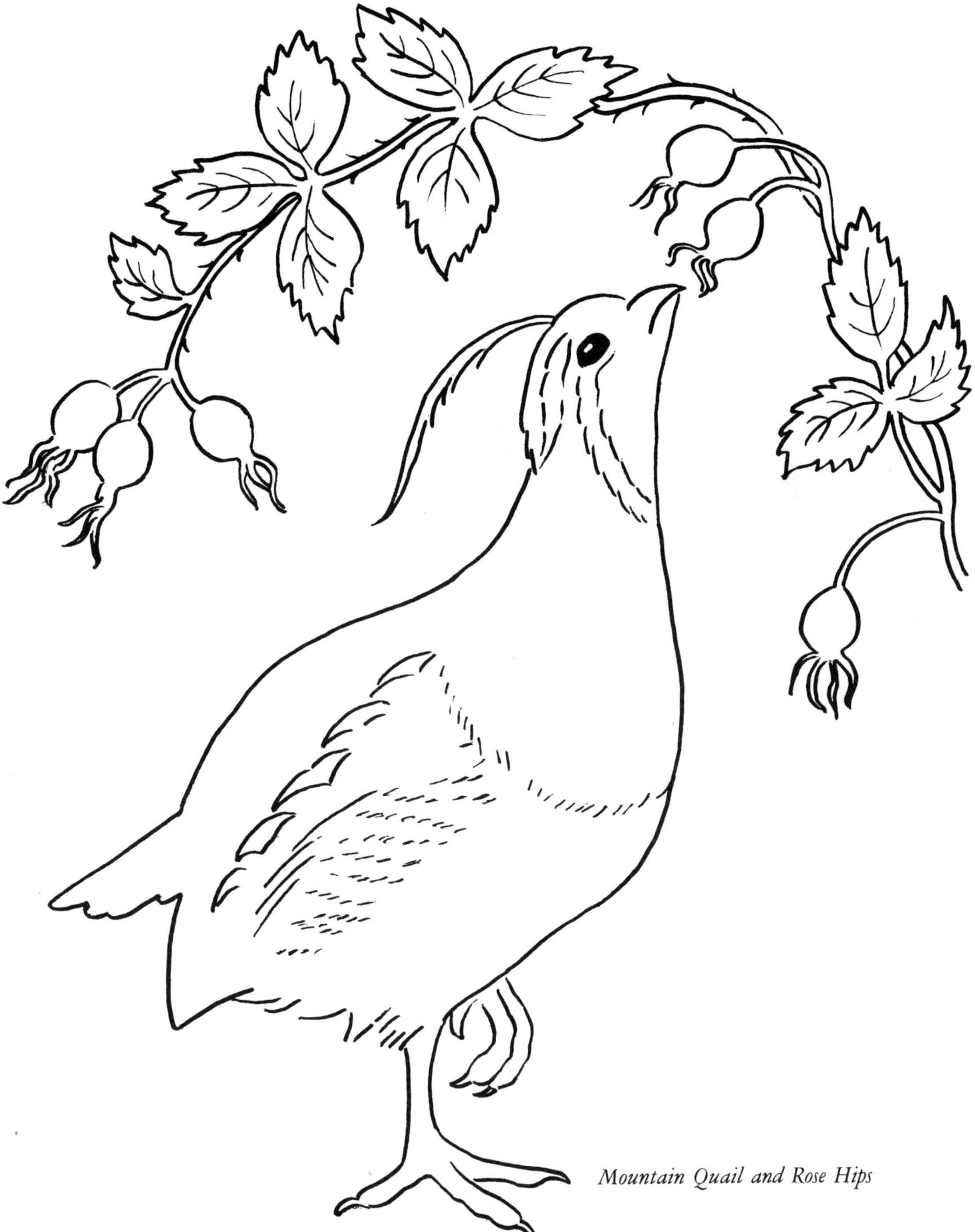

Mountain Quail and Rose Hips

HUMMINGBIRD AND INDIAN PAINTBRUSH

The plaque is constructed by nailing four strips of bark slab to a 9″ by 12″ piece of plywood. Lightly stain with walnut, and rub a small amount of yellow ocher on the background. Trace the design.

The colors used for the bird are: wings, yellow ocher and white; eye and tail, black; breast, white; throat, cadmium red medium; back and head, cadmium yellow light with a touch of thalo blue. The flowers are cadmium red, with cadmium yellow added for highlights. The foliage is thalo blue and cadmium yellow.

Strengthen the design with an outline of black on the shadow side.

Hummingbird and Indian Paintbrush Plaque

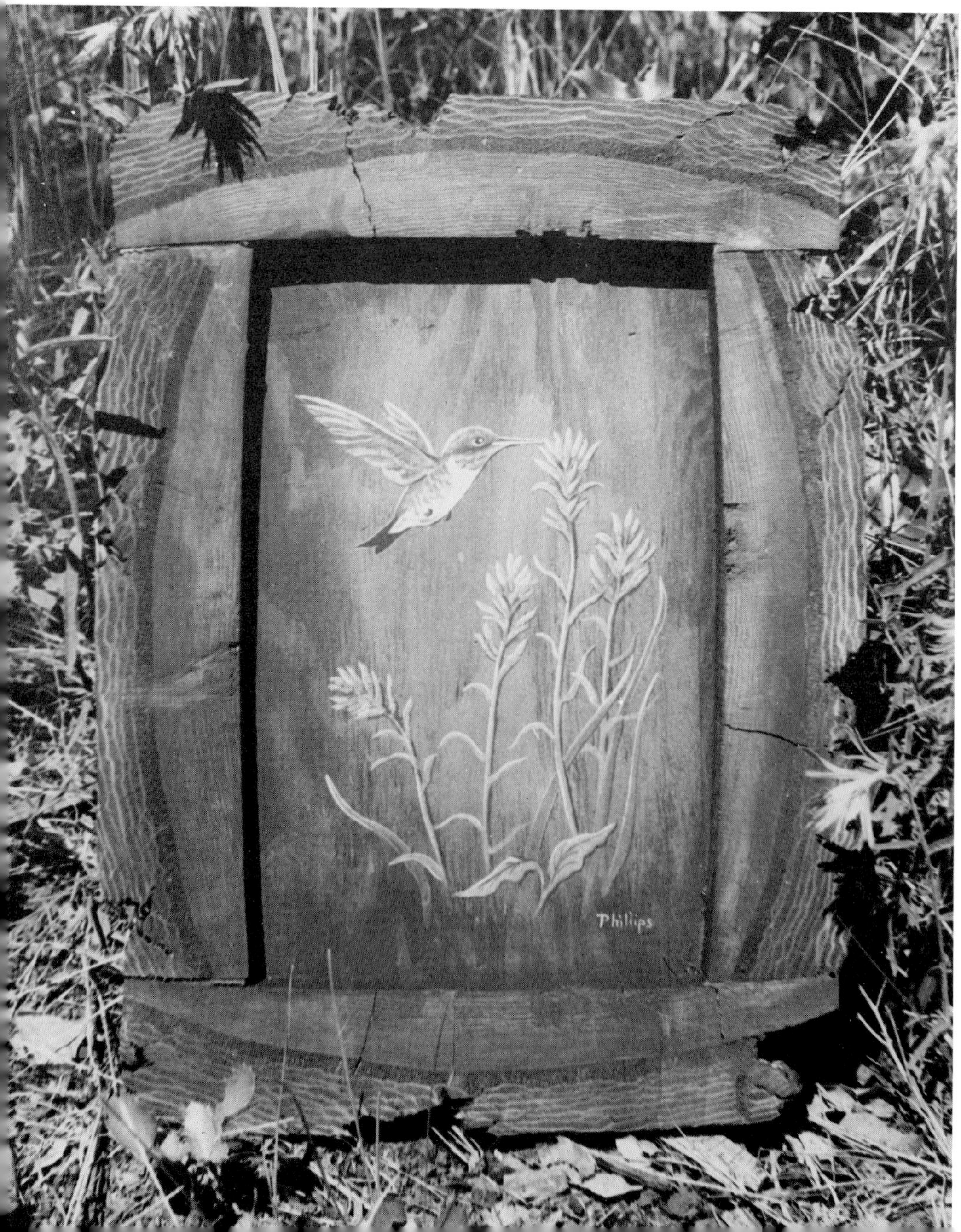

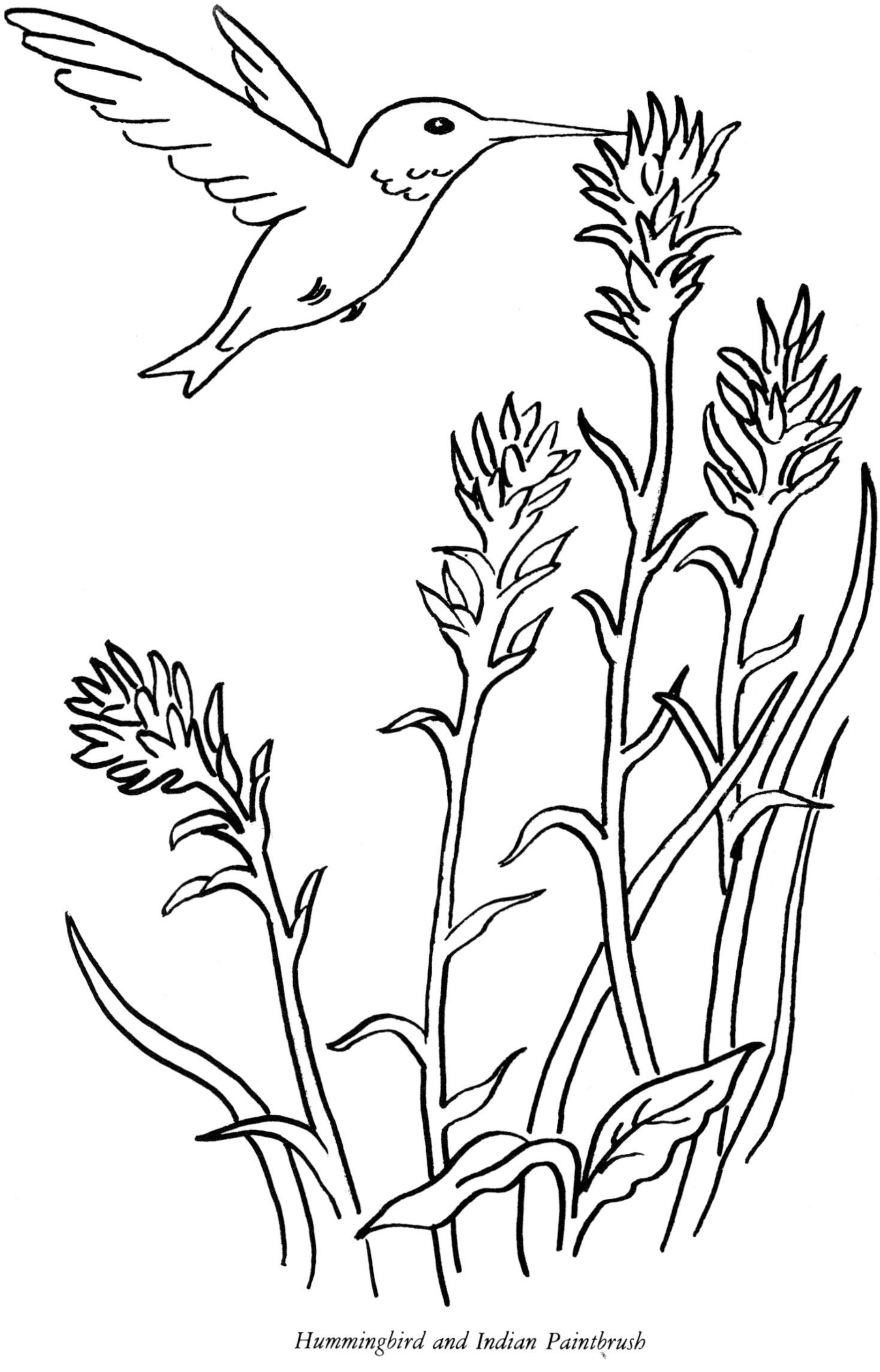

Hummingbird and Indian Paintbrush

6

Other Painting Surfaces

VINYL

A smooth vinyl surface is a joy to paint with acrylics. There are numerous items right in your own home that you can decorate: notebook covers, place mats, overnight bags or purses, and scrapbook covers such as the one pictured here.

MOUNTAIN FLOWERS

The purse is a lasting souvenir of a wild-flower walk in a mountain meadow. I carried my purse, a few tubes of paint, brushes, and a thermos of water. Wherever I met a new flower species, I stopped and "collected" it by painting it on my purse. The bouquet is made up of lupine, scarlet gilia, yellow daisy, bluebell, and the tiny calico flower.

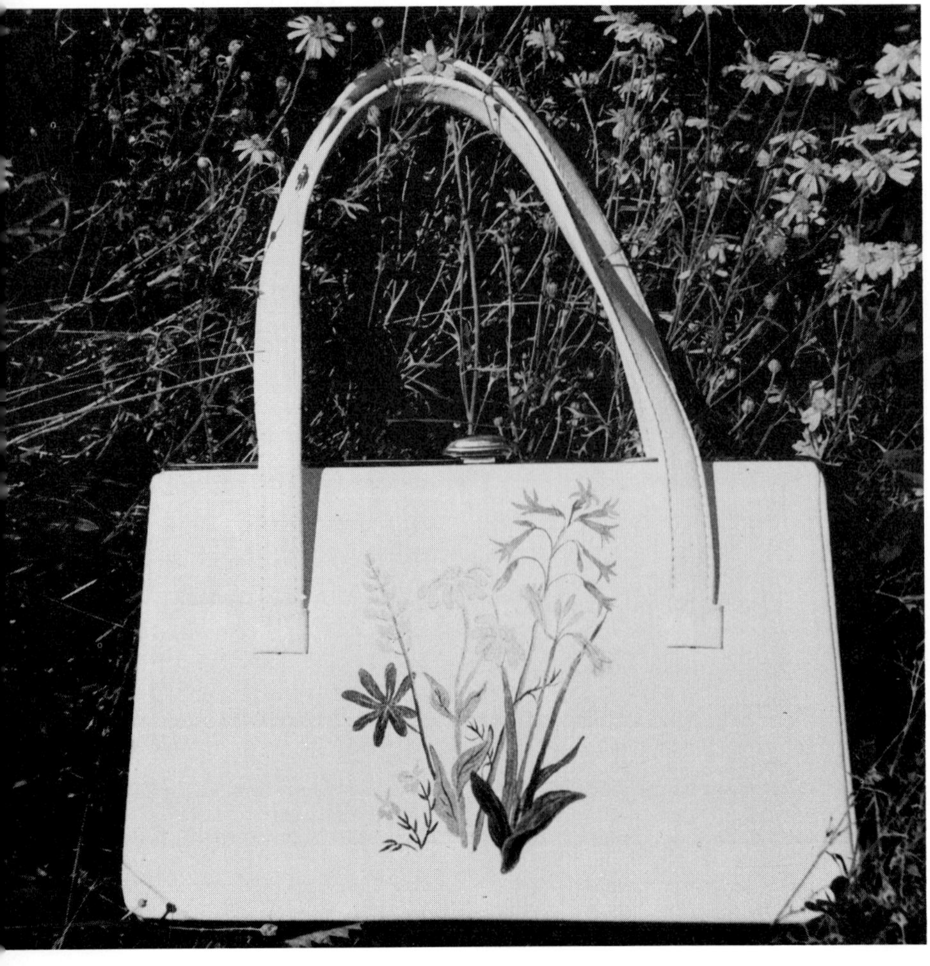

Vinyl Purse with Mountain Flowers

MOUNTAIN LILY

On a wooded hillside was found the mountain lily pictured on this scrapbook cover. These white lilies gradually shade to a deep pink with age, and one stalk carries many shades. The pink was made by mixing white and Naphthol crimson.

Scrapbook with Mountain Lily

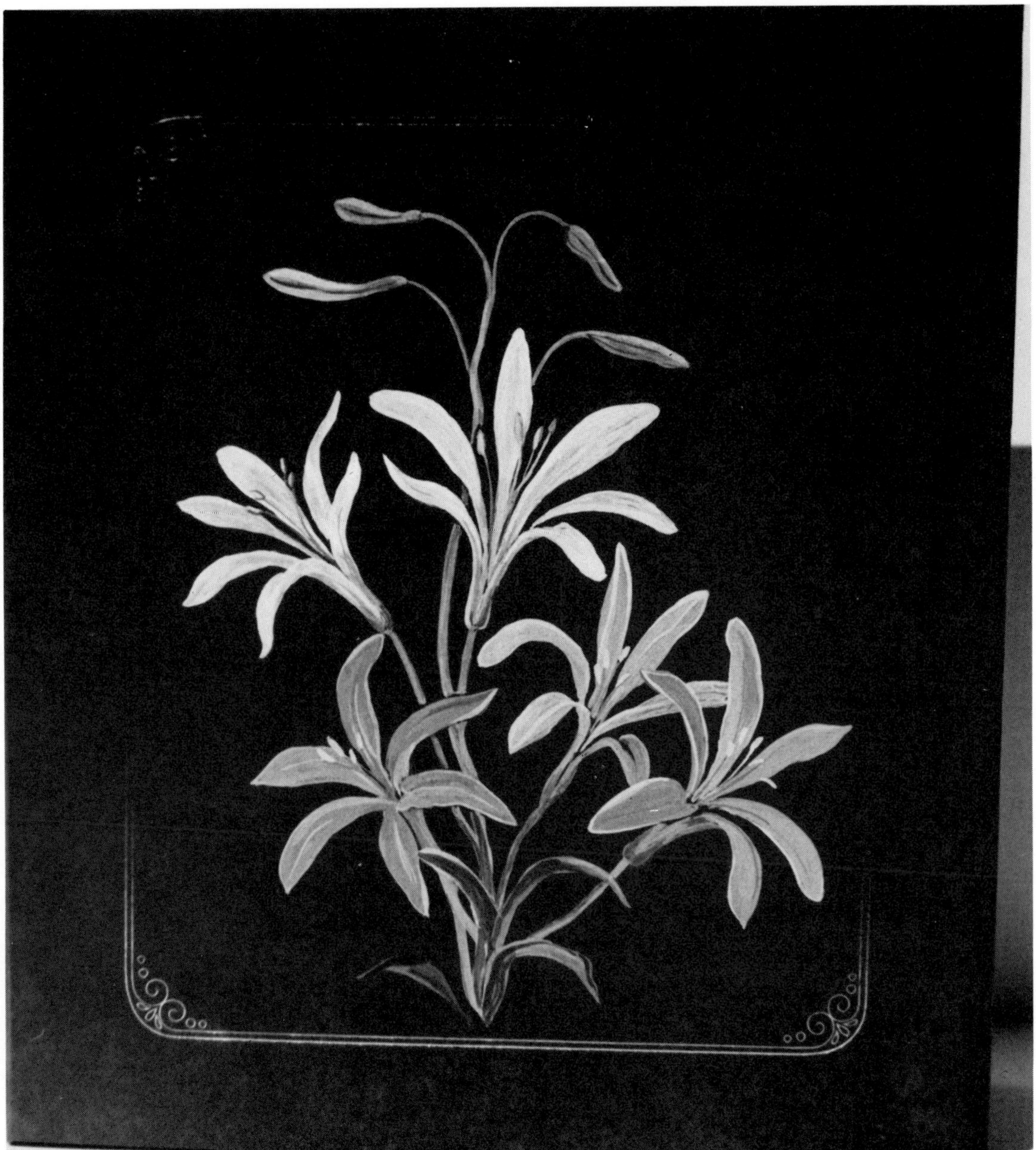

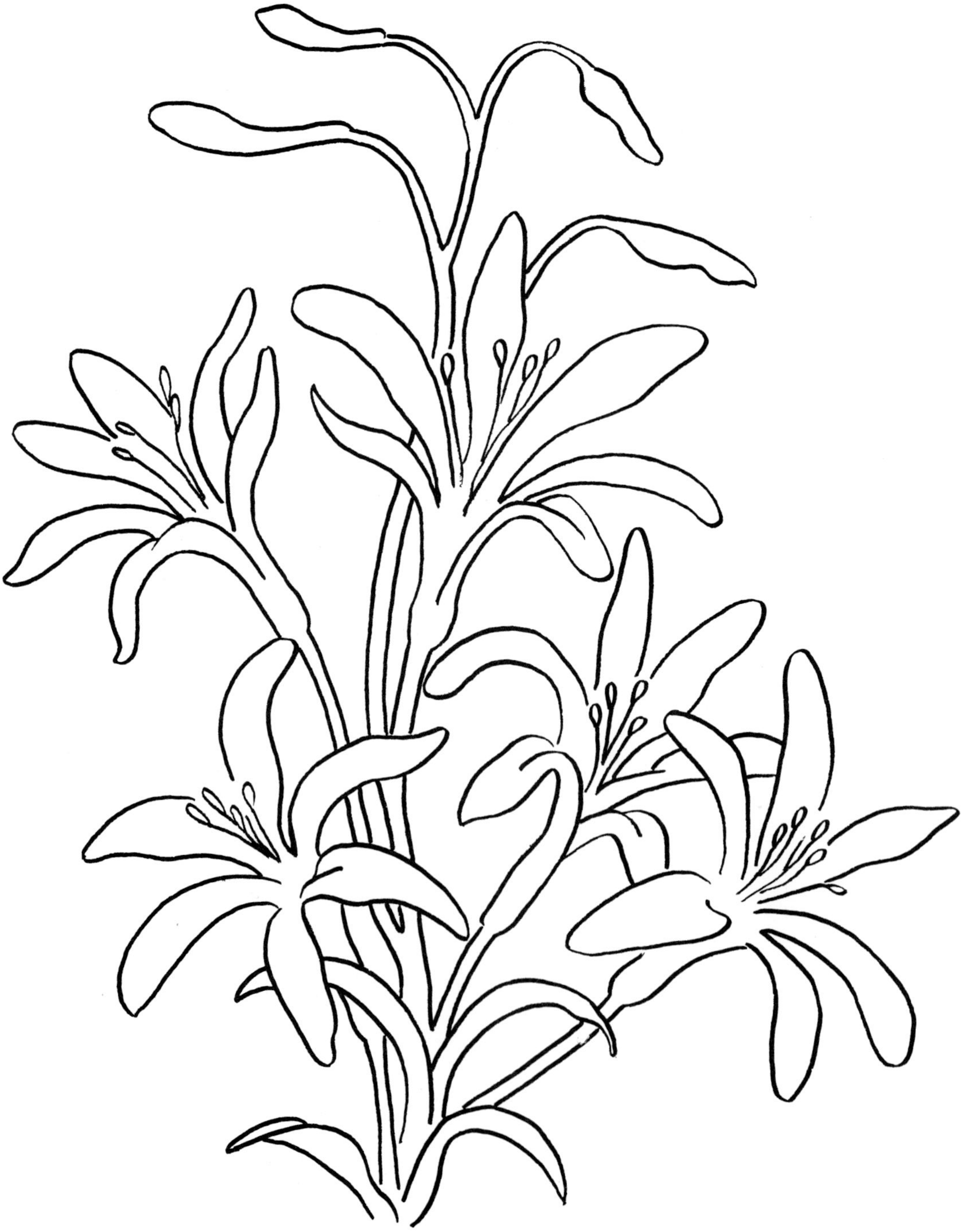

Mountain Lily

FABRIC

Acrylic painted on fabric is permanent; if reasonable care is used in laundering, it will not wash out. A smooth polyester material works best for this. The possibilities are numerous: blouses, T-shirts, table napkins, place mats, curtains, or dresser scarfs such as the one shown here.

Draw your design lightly with pencil. If the material is quite sheer, the pattern may be placed underneath the material and traced.

Experiment first on a scrap of material before painting your best blouse. Use a pointed bristle brush to apply the first coat of paint; a flat sable brush is fine for shading over a painted area. Do not put paint on too thickly, but do not dilute it too thinly or the color will bleed. Move the brush loaded with paint back and forth over the fabric in a scrubbing motion to get the paint down into the threads. Keep your design simple!

FIELD FLOWERS

The flowers on the dresser scarf are: lupine, columbine, bellflowers, sunflower, and buttercups. The colors used are: cadmium yellow medium, cadmium yellow deep, yellow ocher, burnt umber, cadmium red light, thalo blue, and white.

Dresser Scarf with Field Flowers

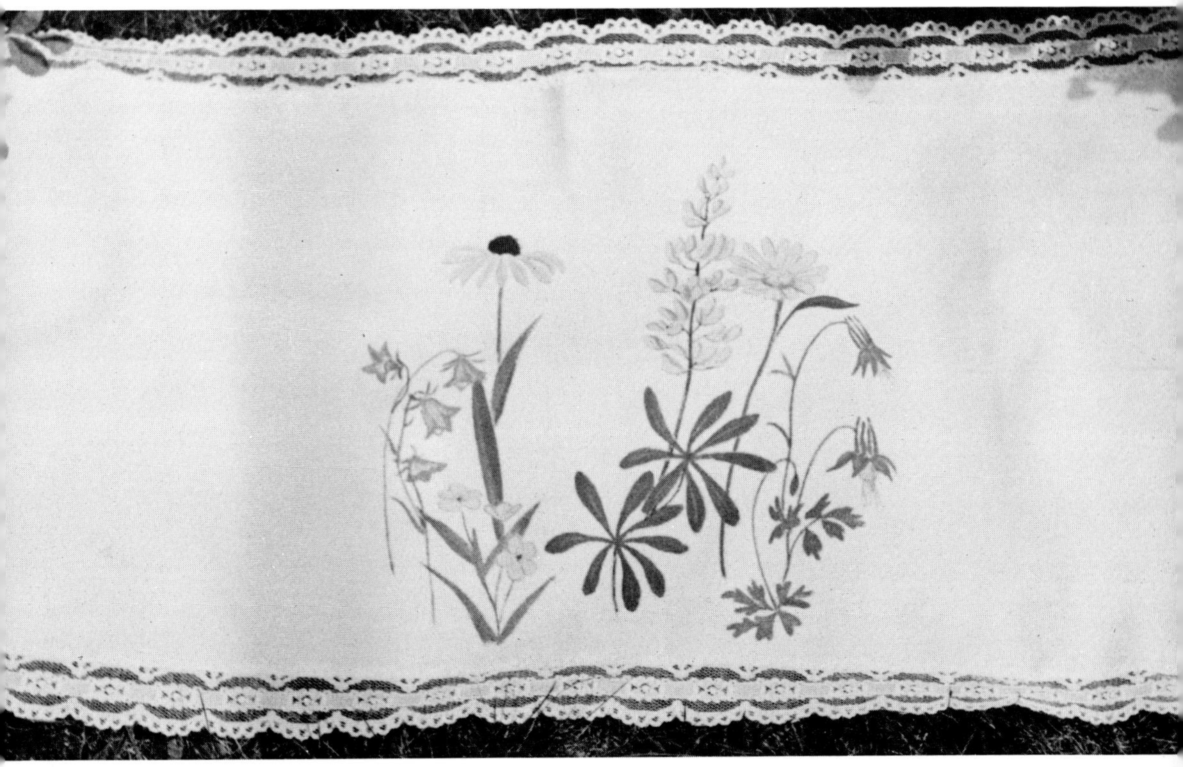

Field Flowers

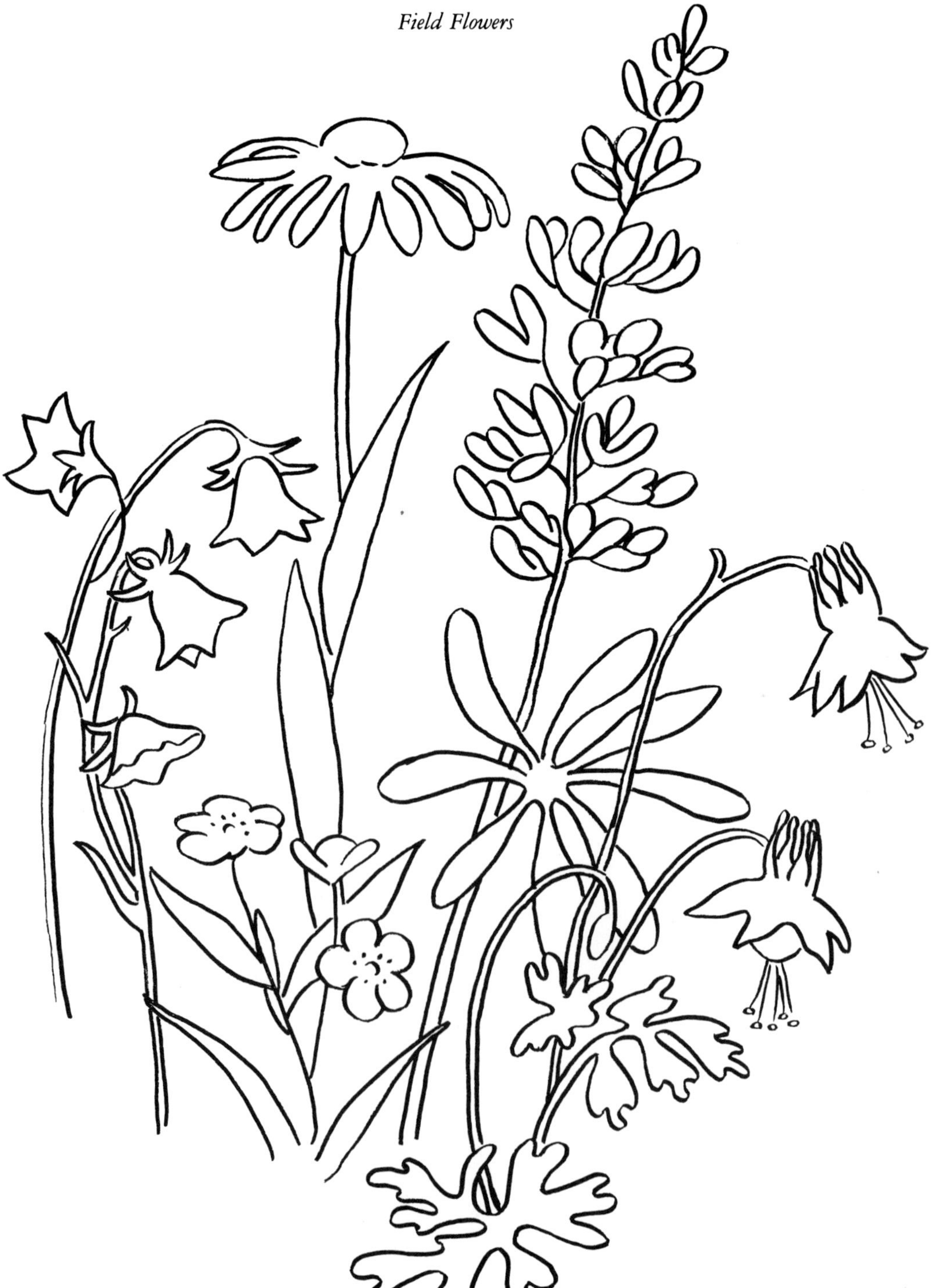

CORK

Fine- or medium-grained cork is a good painting surface, needs no preparation, and lends itself to many possibilities: coasters, trivets, bulletin boards. No final glaze is needed. Trace on the pattern with carbon.

FROG AND VIOLETS

Frog: shades of green made with cadmium yellow and thalo blue, orange eye. Outline the frog with black.

Violets: purple (made with red and blue) and white; leaves and stems, thalo blue and cadmium yellow, white added for highlights.

Ladybug, cadmium red.

Cork Trivet with Frog and Violets

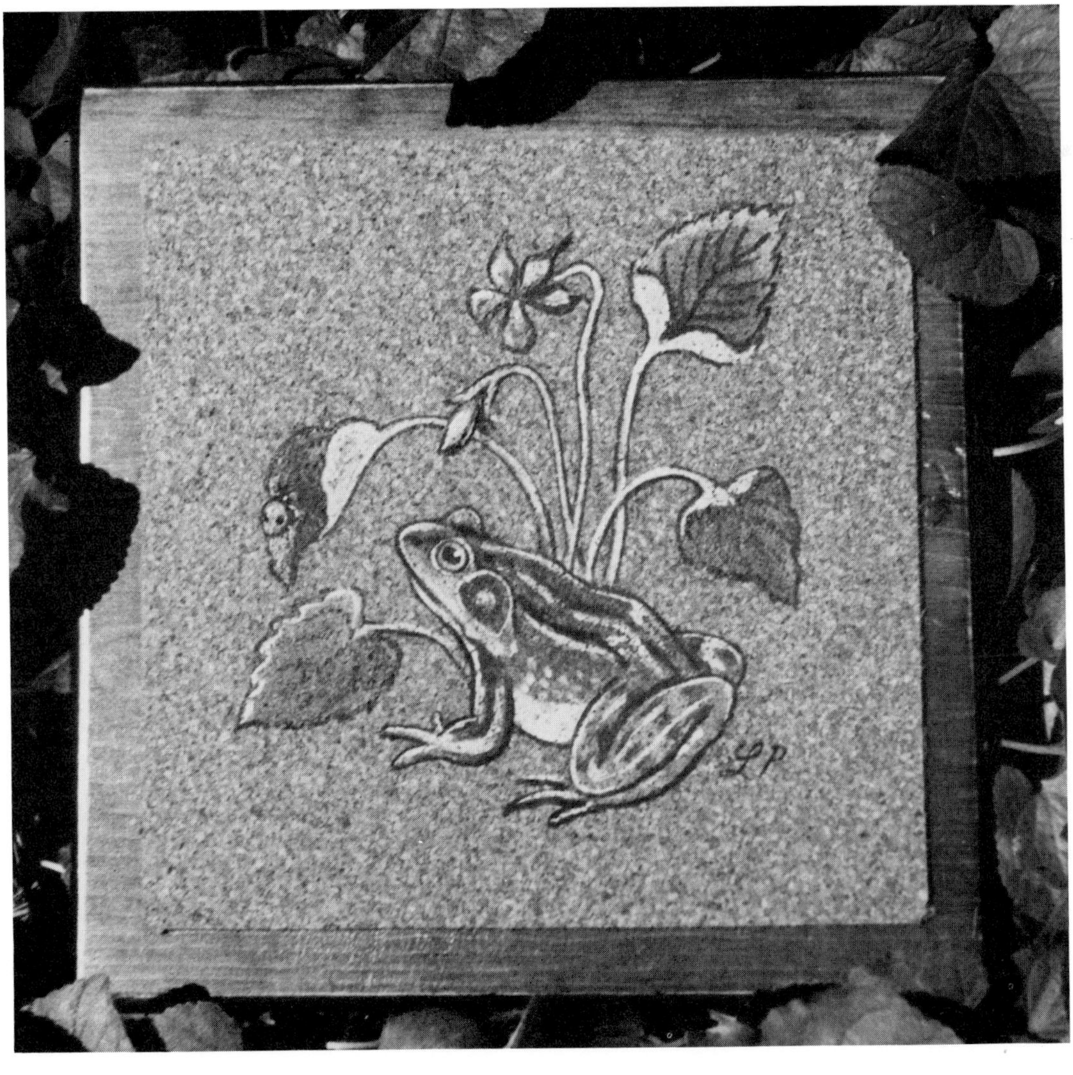

Frog and Violets

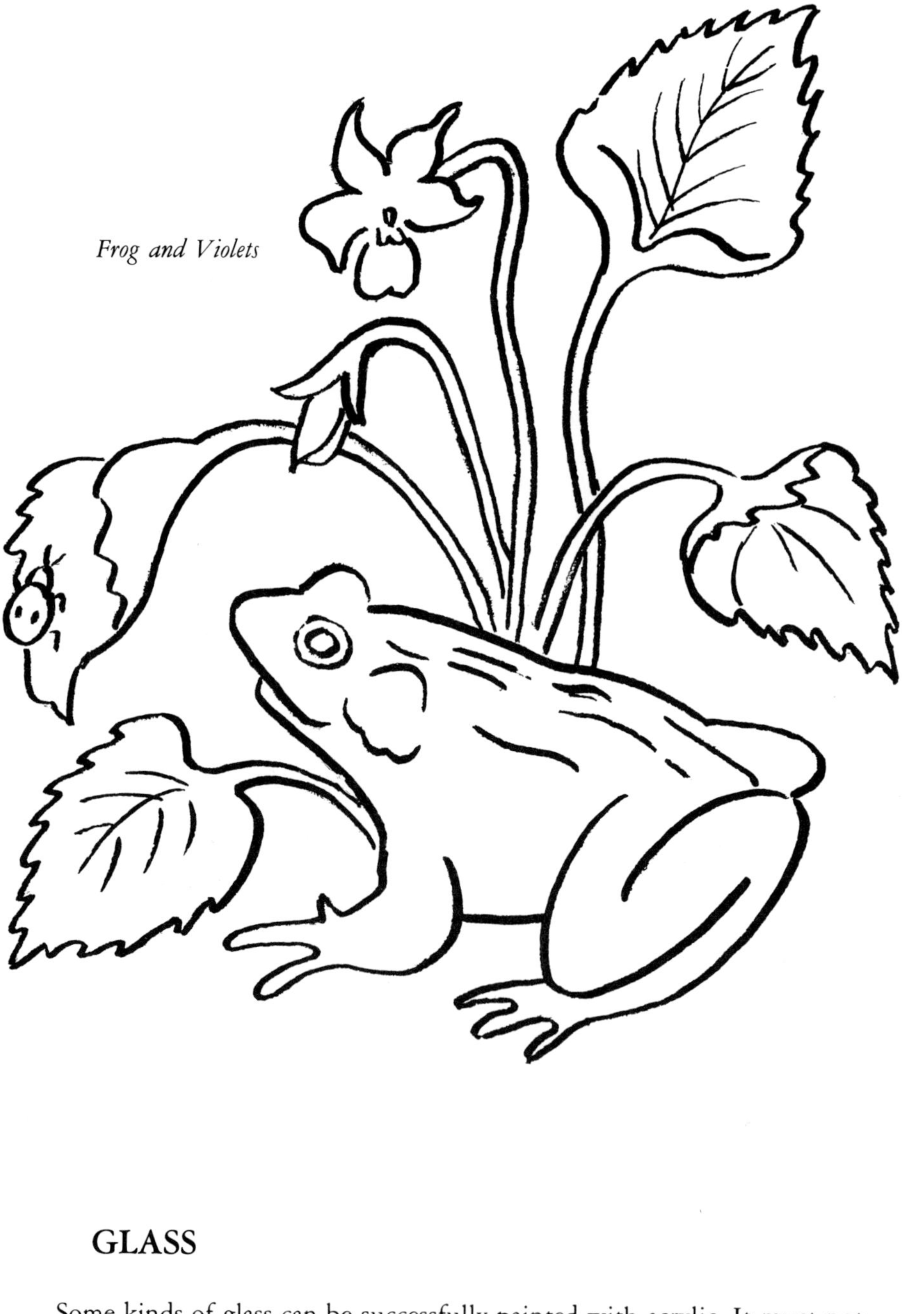

GLASS

Some kinds of glass can be successfully painted with acrylic. It must not have a high glaze, such as drinking glasses have. Choose glass with a soft mat finish and an item that will not require frequent immersion in water.

WILD FLAX

The lampshade was painted freehand, since tracing a design on glass is difficult. Keep the pattern of your design before you as a guide when doing this. It may be possible to tape the design to the inside of the glass and work over it.

The wild flax is thalo blue and white.

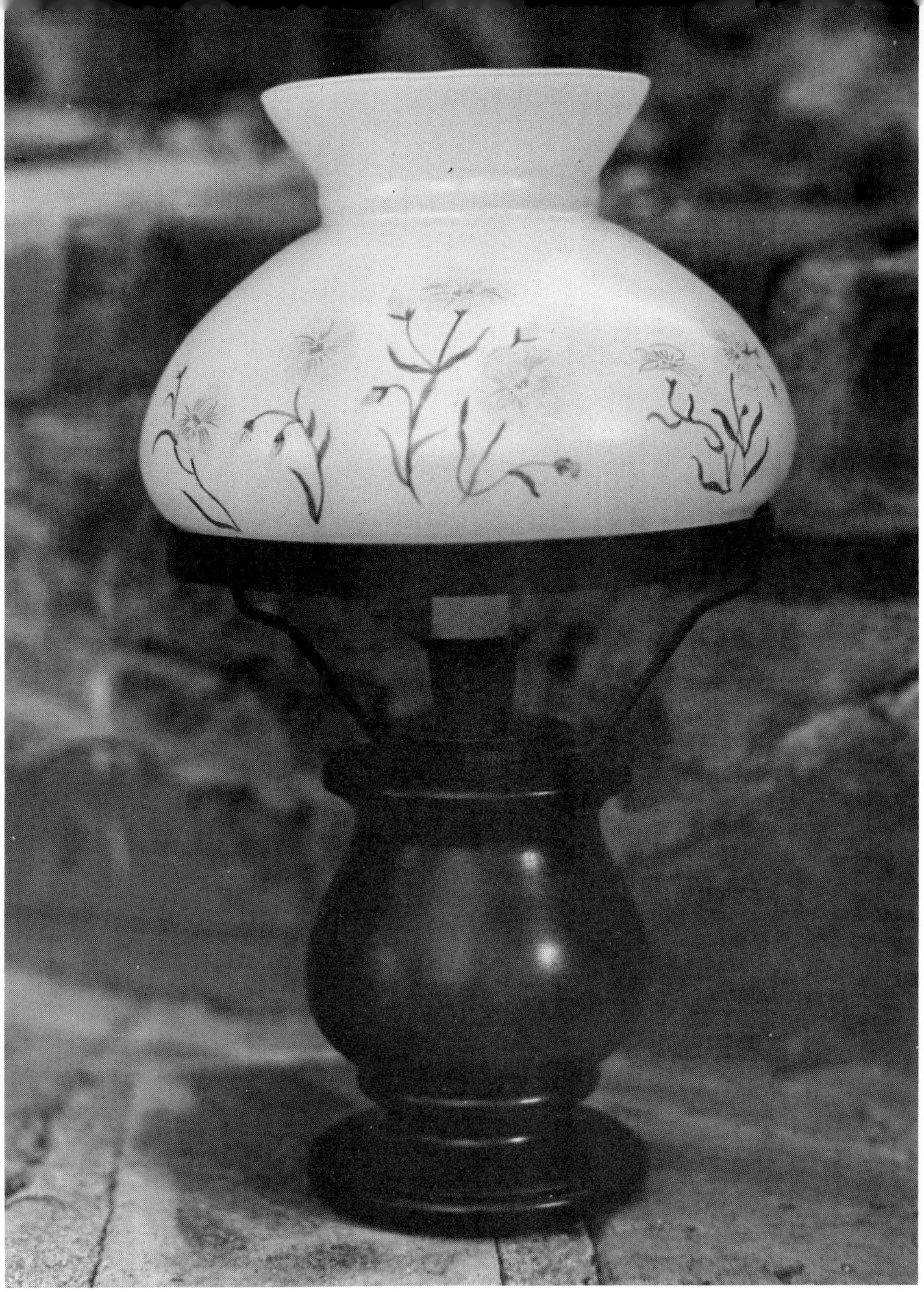

Hurricane Lamp with Wild Flax

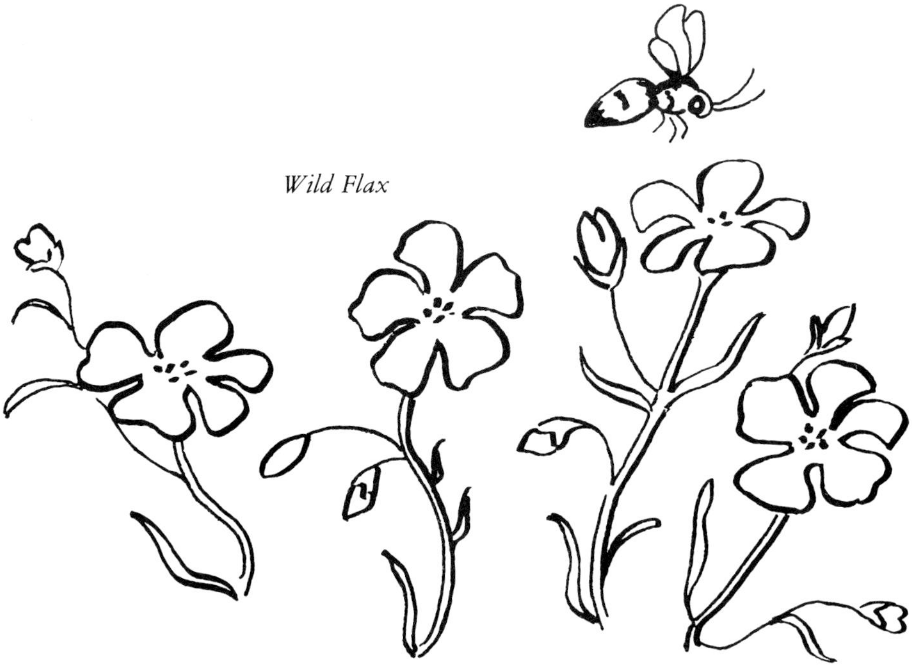

Wild Flax

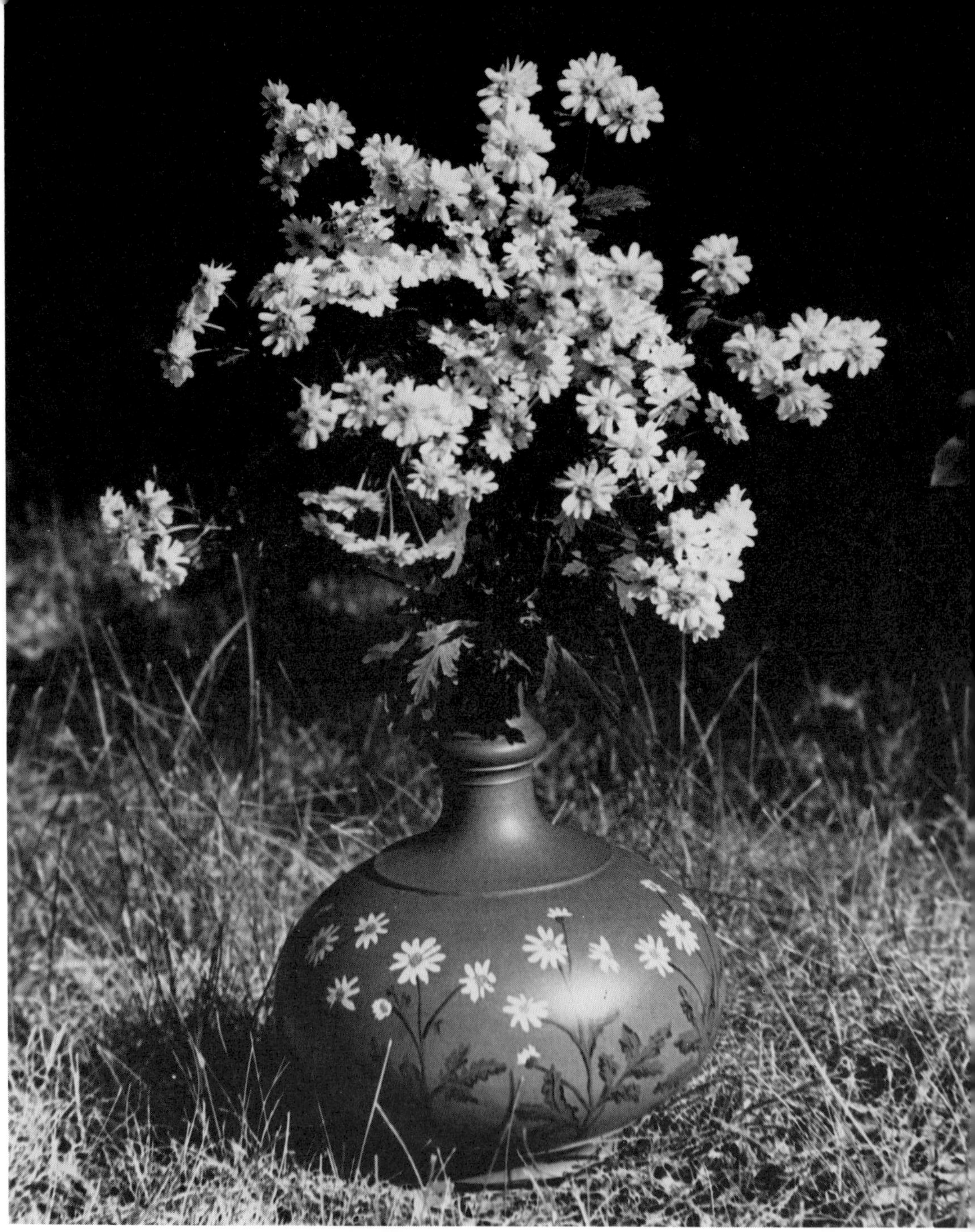

Clay Jar with Wild Chrysanthemums

UNGLAZED POTTERY

WILD CHRYSANTHEMUMS

Flowerpots and jars of unglazed pottery clay have good, paintable surfaces. They require no preparation before painting. You may find it easiest to draw your design on in pencil. It may also be traced on with carbon, but often a round surface makes this impractical and it must be painted freehand.

The vase shown here was given a light gloss with a spray can of clear acrylic varnish. Clay is highly absorbent and the varnish darkens it considerably. It is well to keep this in mind, for parts of your design may be lost in varnishing.

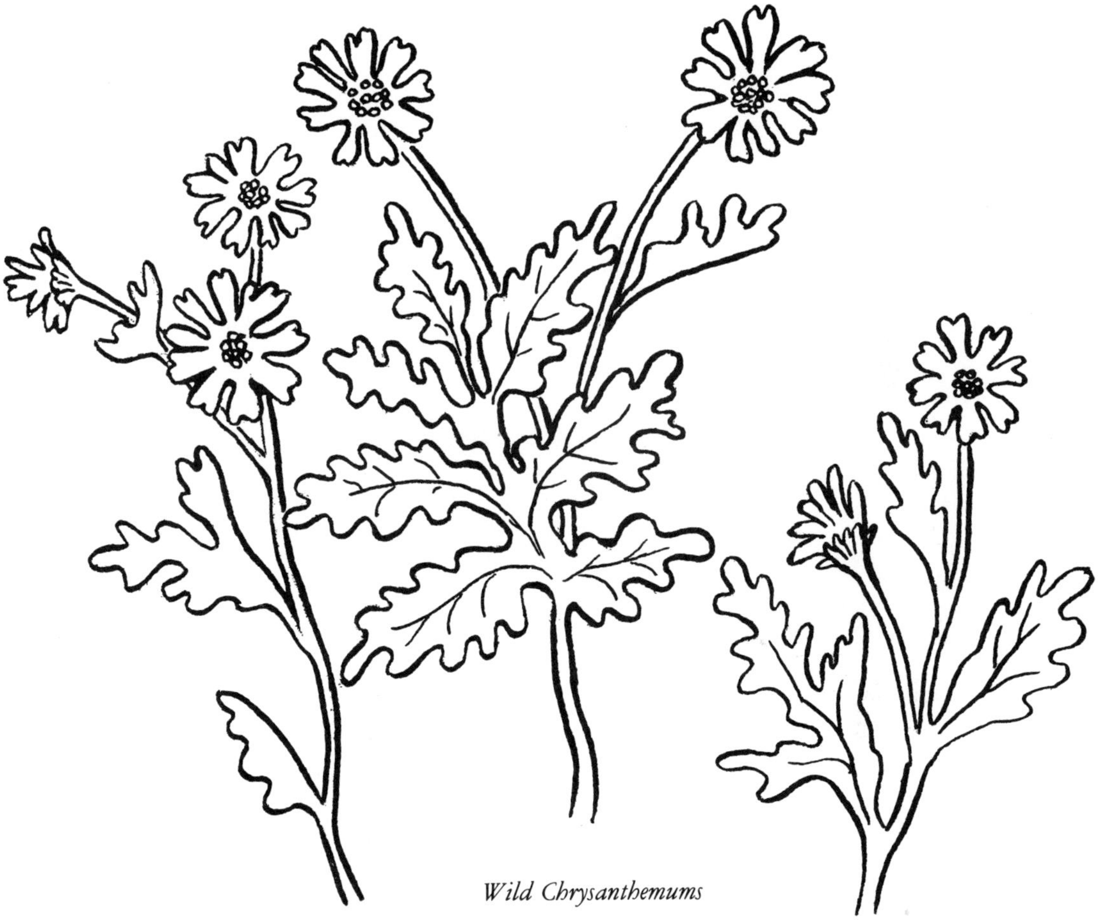

Wild Chrysanthemums

ROCK OWLS

Pebbles tumbled smooth by ocean waters or mountain streams are fun to paint. Large ones can be used as paperweights; smaller ones may be glued on to a plaque or displayed on pieces of driftwood.

No preparation or finish is needed for the stones. Simply paint them in bright colors. Add bits of driftwood and dried moss for a plaque.

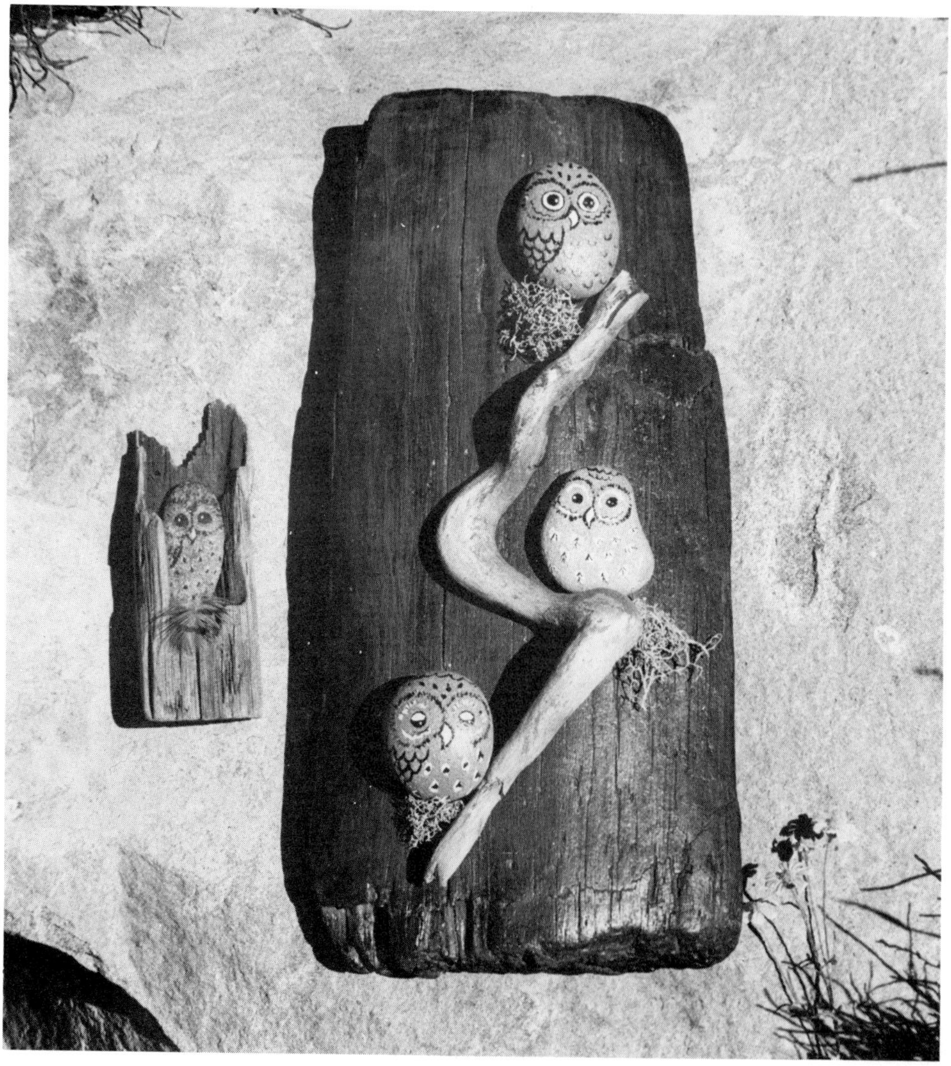

Rock Owls

METAL

Metal items with an enamel finish can be successfully painted with acrylics. An example is the folding chair shown here, which may be purchased in a variety of colors, already finished, and lacking only a decorative design.

Use the paint full strength on this, since diluted paint will tend to bead when applied. Keeping your pattern before you for reference, paint on freehand. If you make an error, simply scrape it off and do it over again. Go over the design twice; the second time is for highlighting. When the design is finished, coat with clear acrylic varnish for permanence.

SUNFLOWERS

Colors used:
Cadmium yellow medium for petals: the center is burnt sienna.
The leaves are cadmium yellow and thalo blue.

Metal Folding Chair with Sunflowers

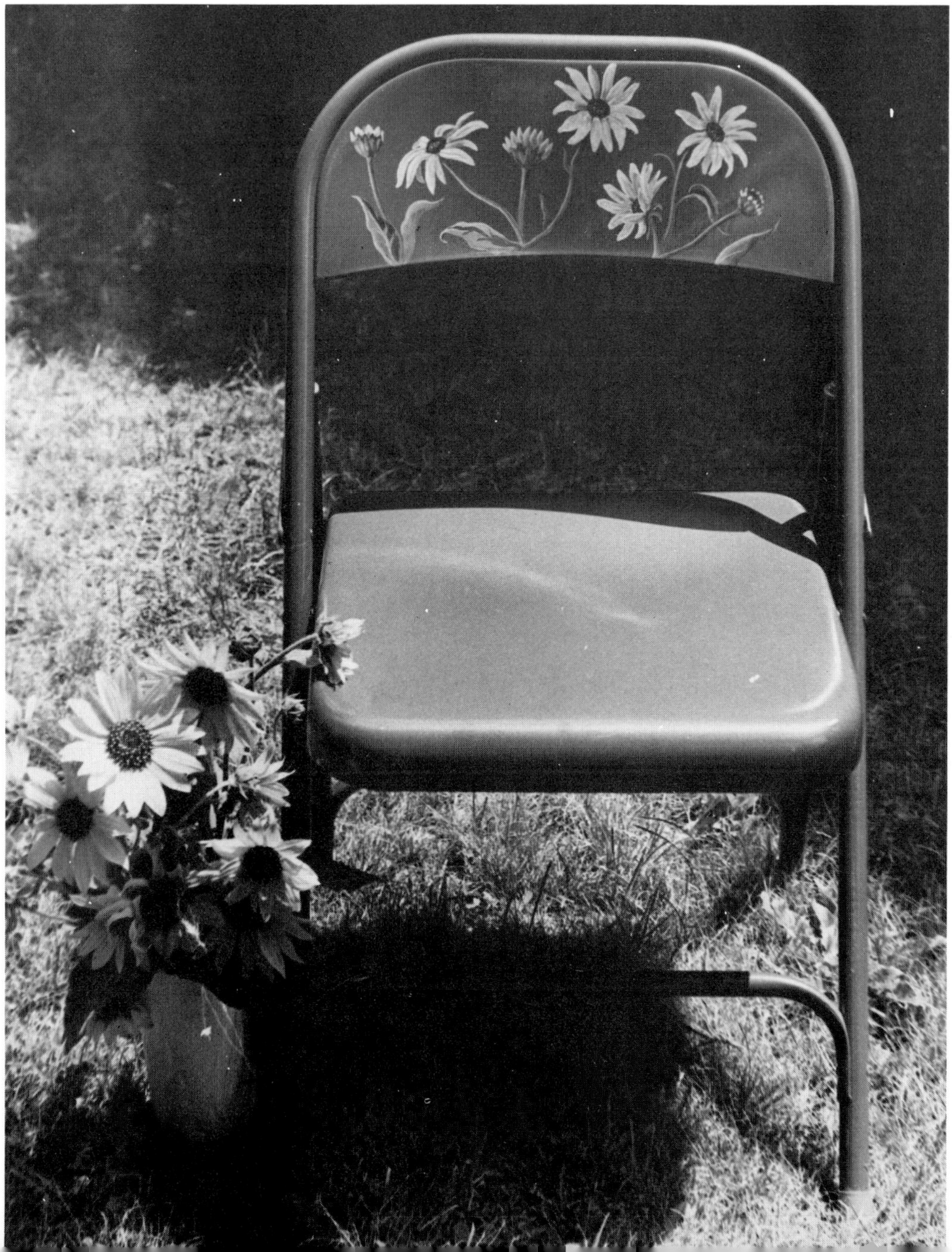

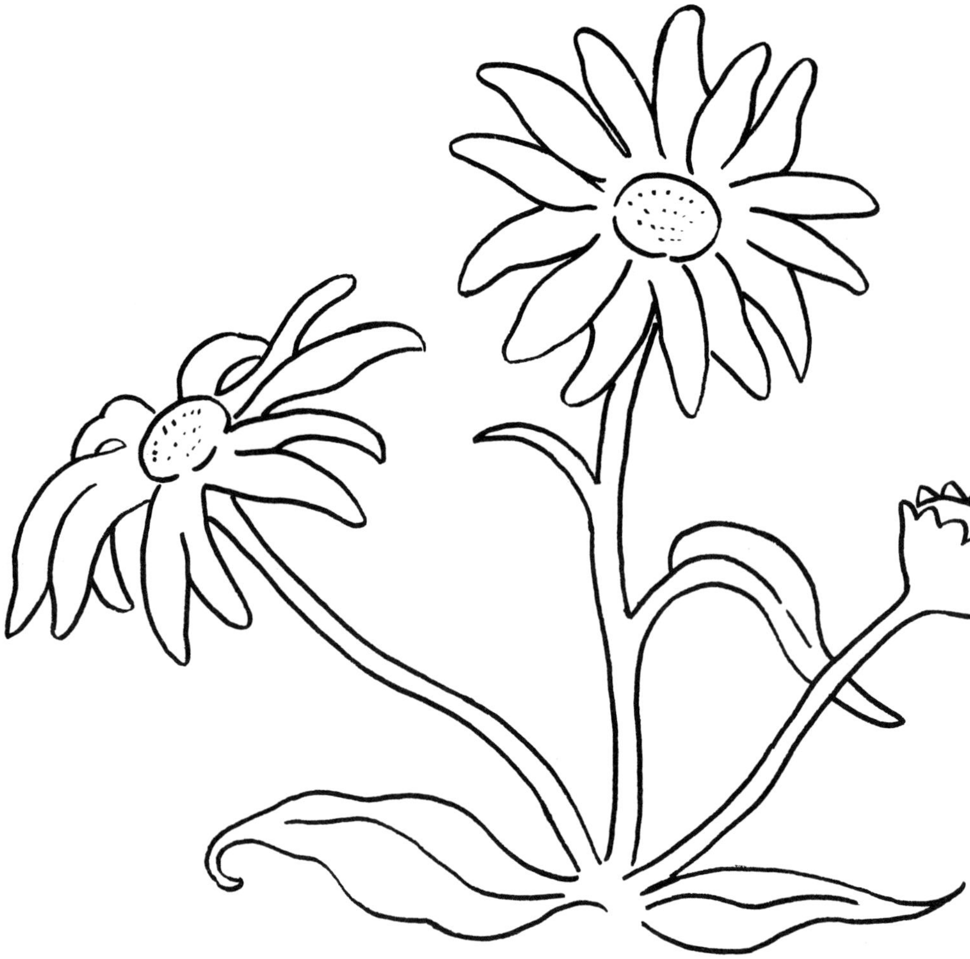

Sunflowers

NATURE BOXES

Here is a chance to use those bits of memorabilia you have collected on walks in the woods.

BLUEBIRD BOX

Paint the design on a small 8″ by 10″ canvas board or heavy cardboard that has been given a coat of gesso. Bluebirds have thalo blue backs and wings and burnt sienna breasts. The baby bird has more gray feathers than the adult. (Use black and white with a dab of blue for the gray.) Mount the painting in a shadow box that has been stained umber. Glue on such items as twigs, pinecones, bark, feathers, and an empty nest. (Eggs are made of clay.)

Bluebird Nature Box

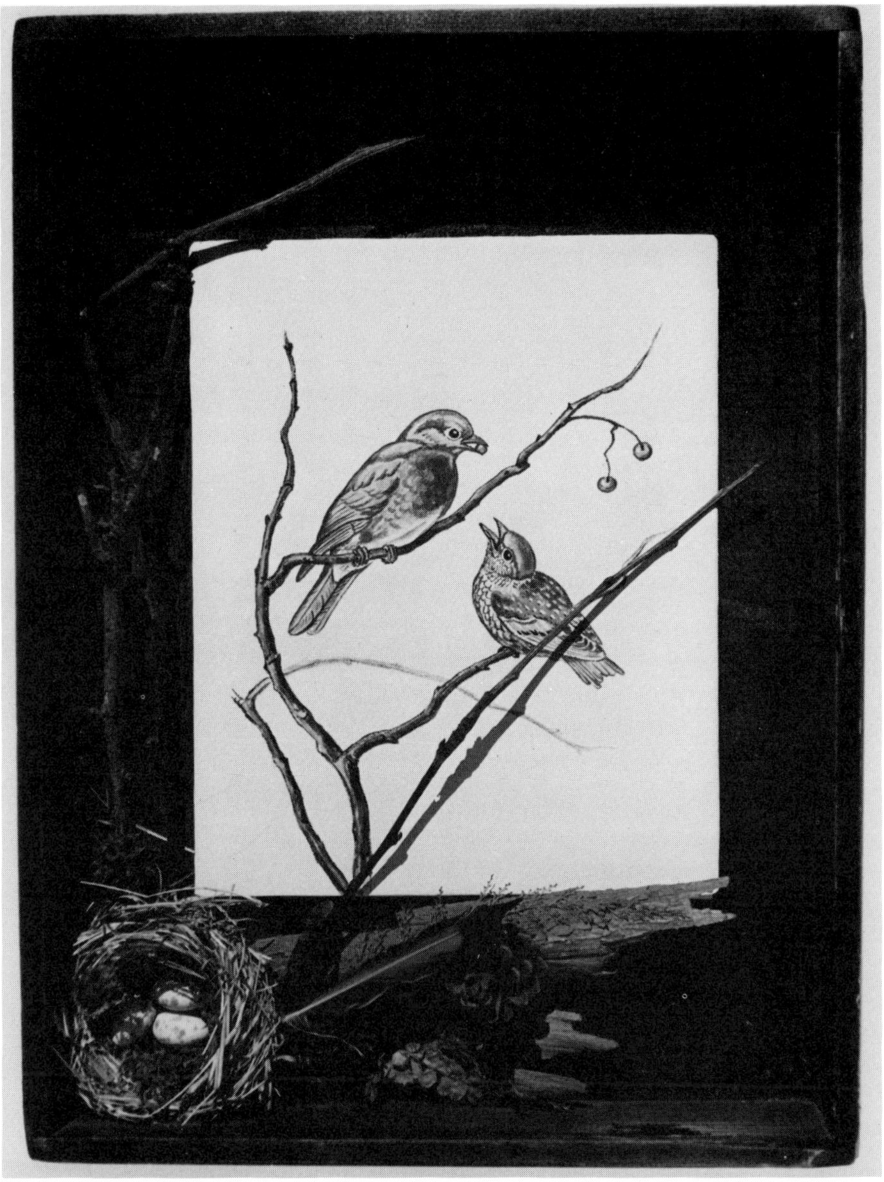

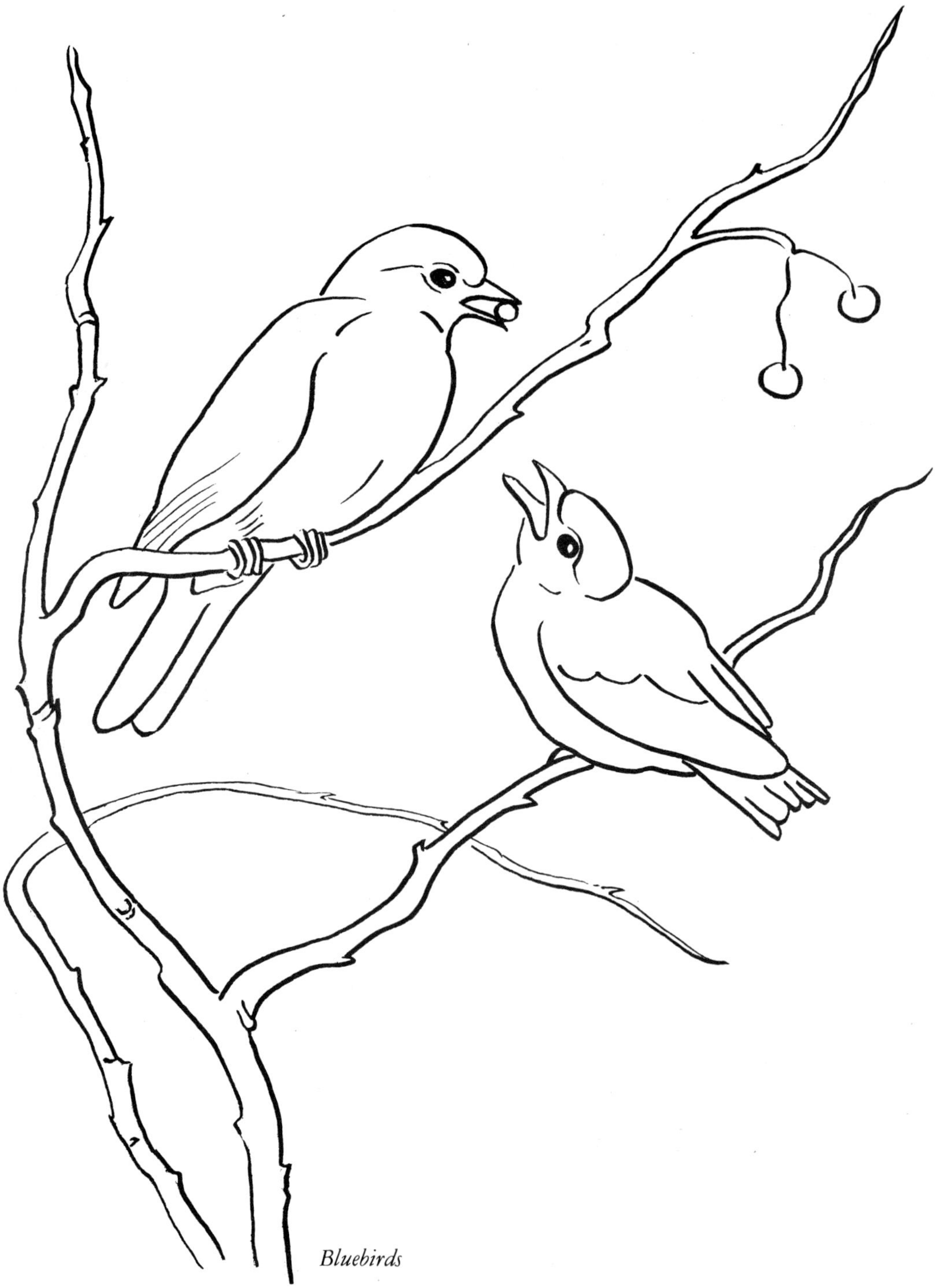

Bluebirds

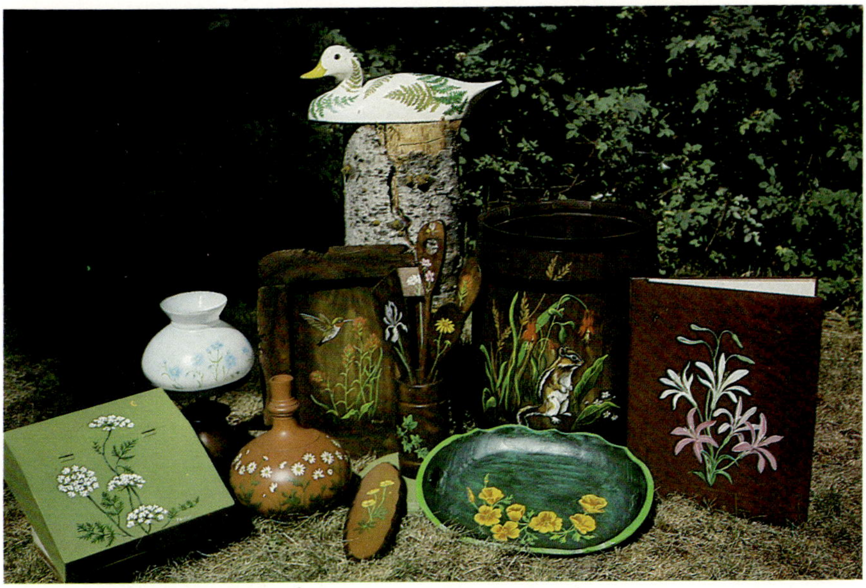

Group of Decorated Crafts

Mountain Quail Plaque

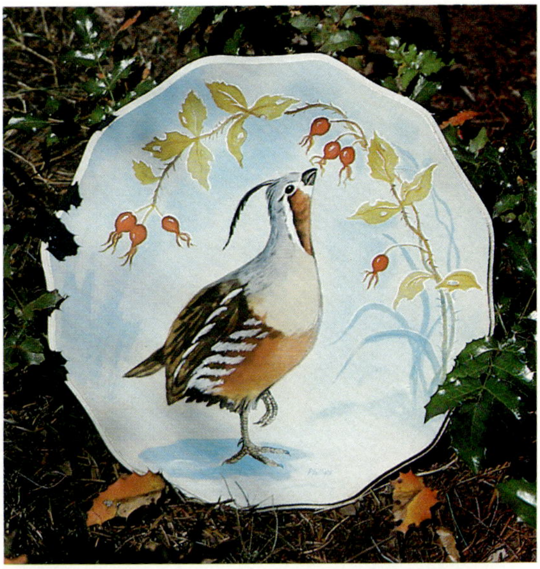

Bottom right: *Decorated Candles*

Below: *Towel Holder with Rabbits*

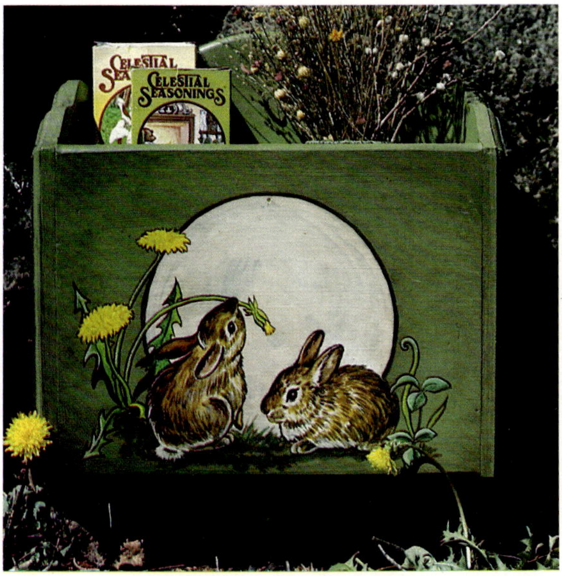

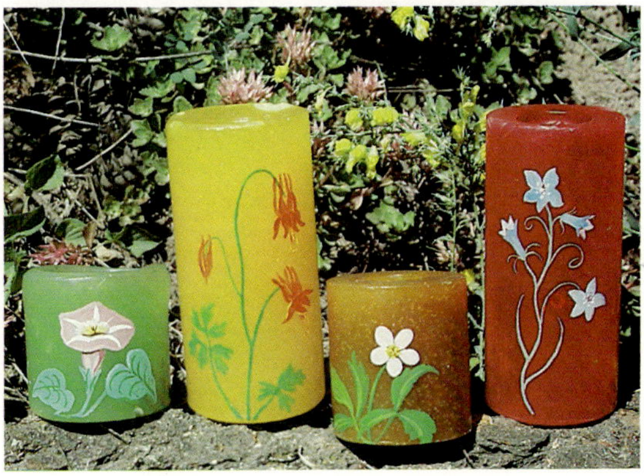

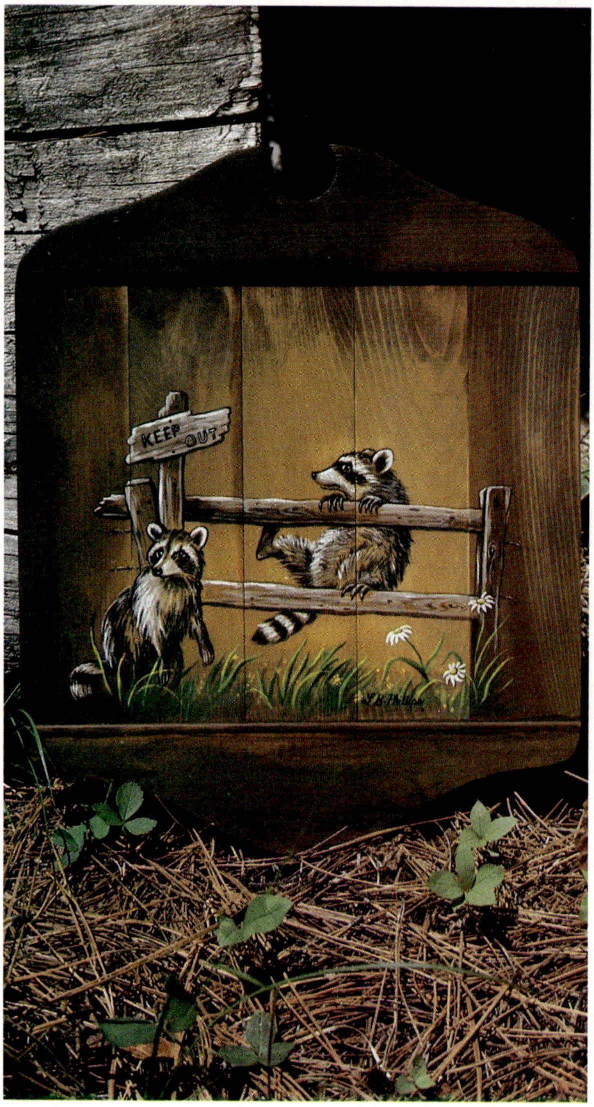

Raccoon Plaque

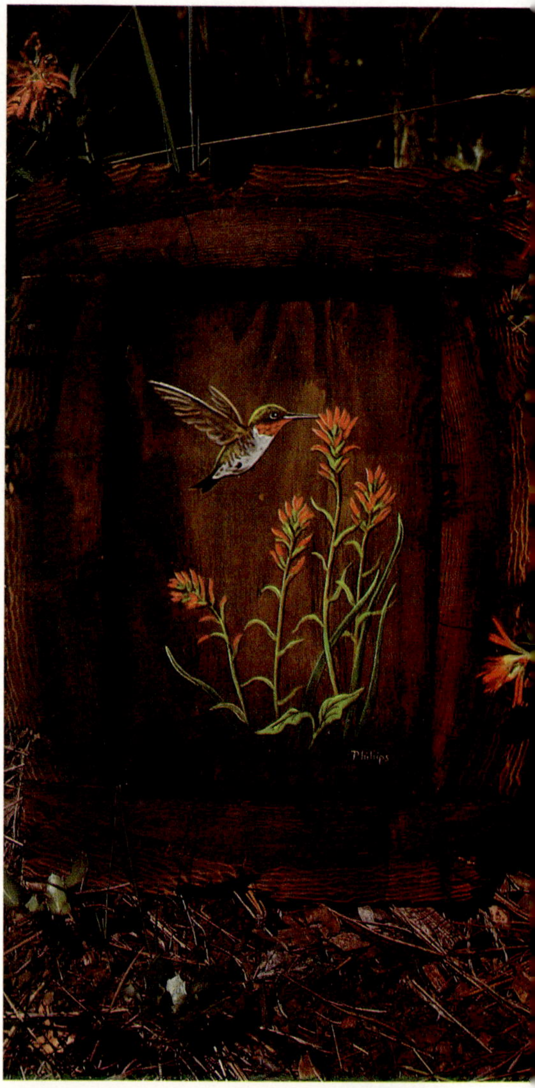

Hummingbird Plaque

Leaf Designs on Pillows

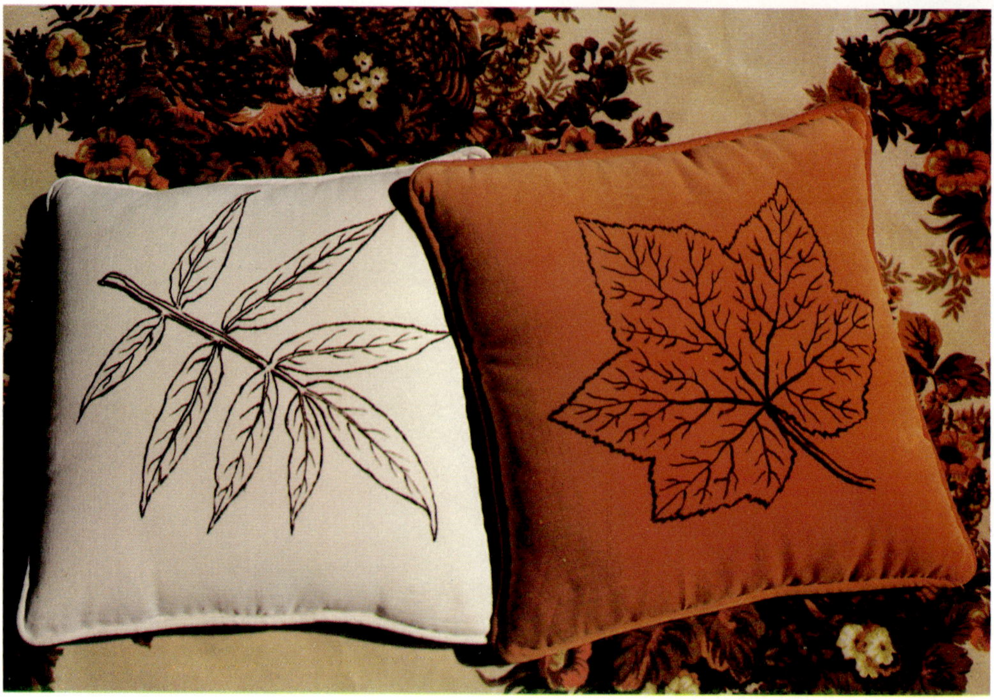

Rock Owls

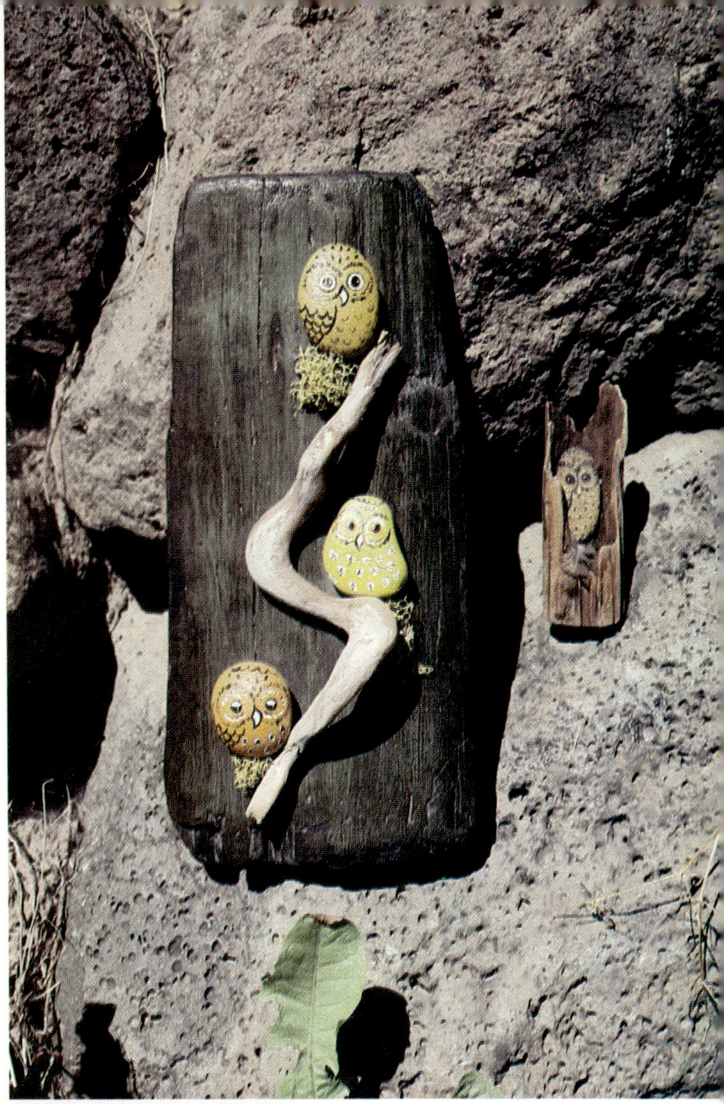

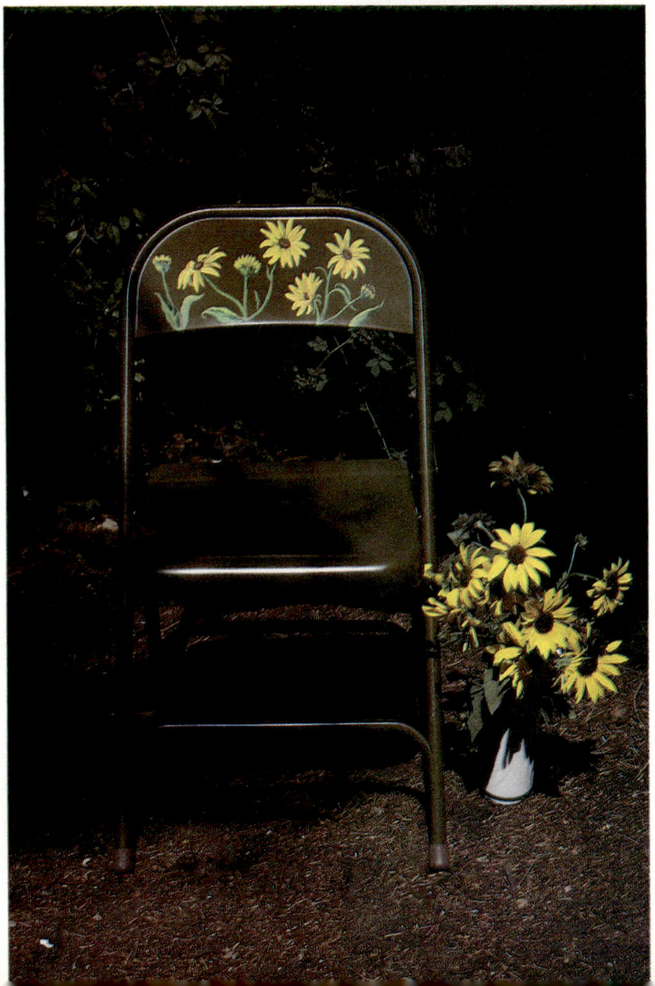

Metal Chair with Sunflowers

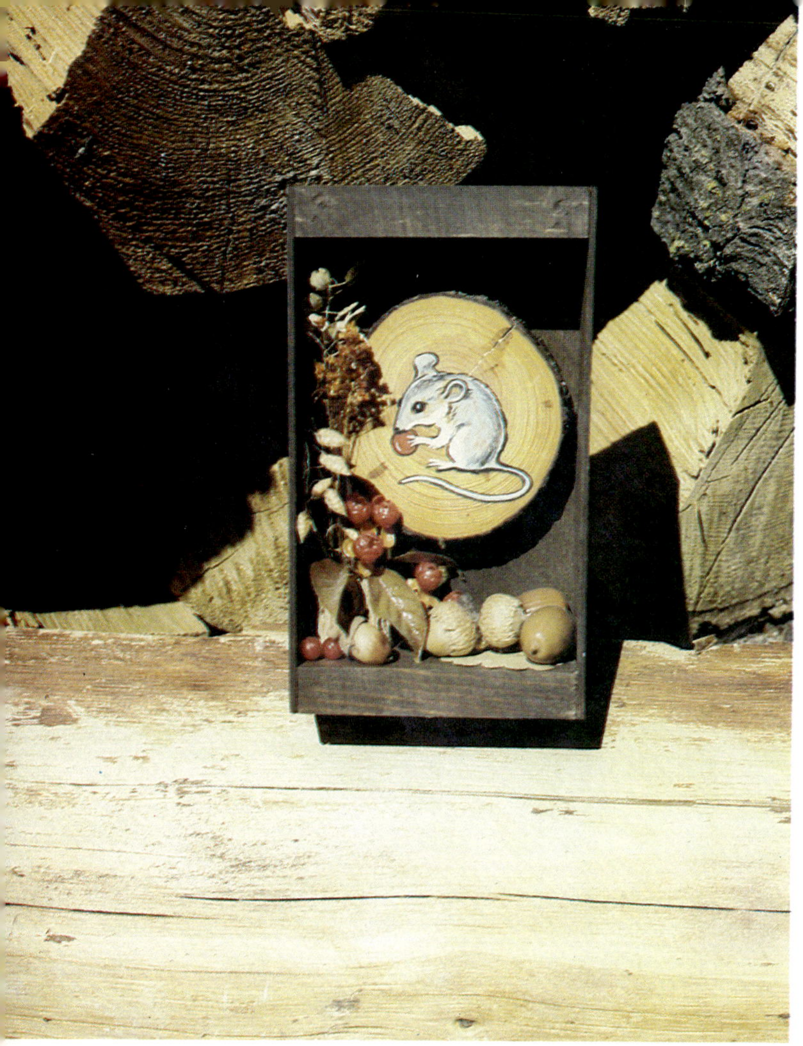

Nature Box: Mouse

Greeting Cards with Pressed Flowers

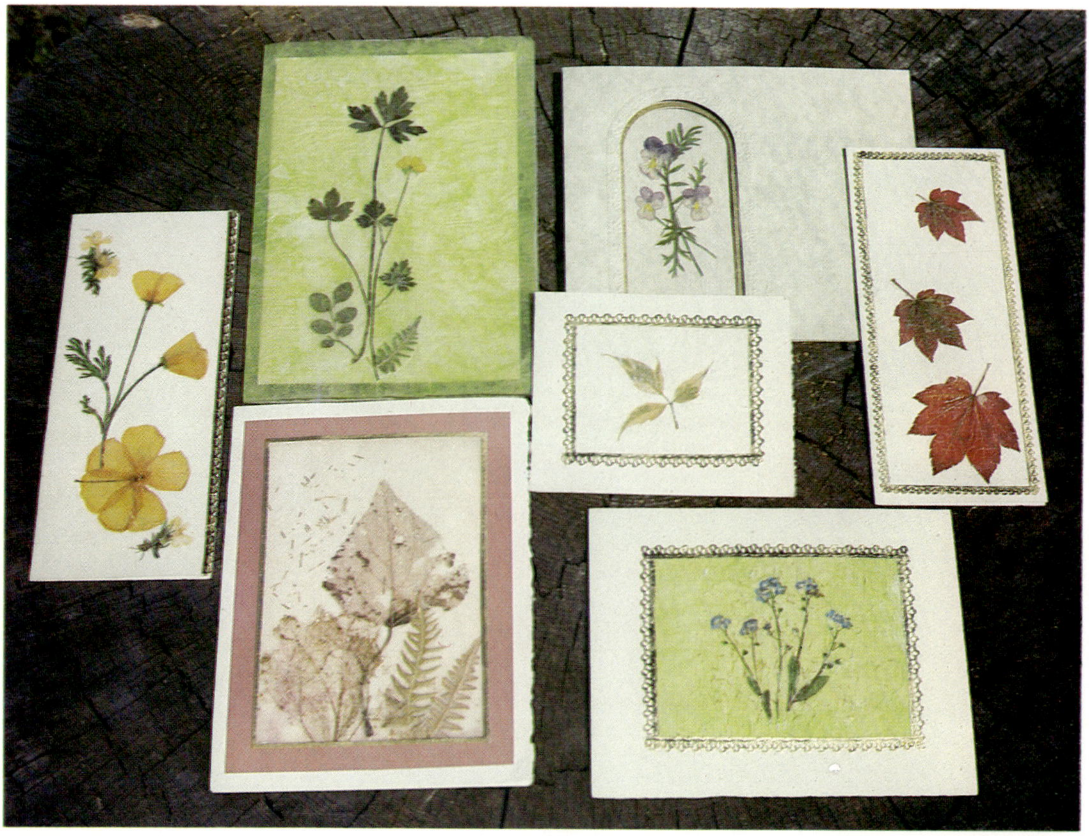

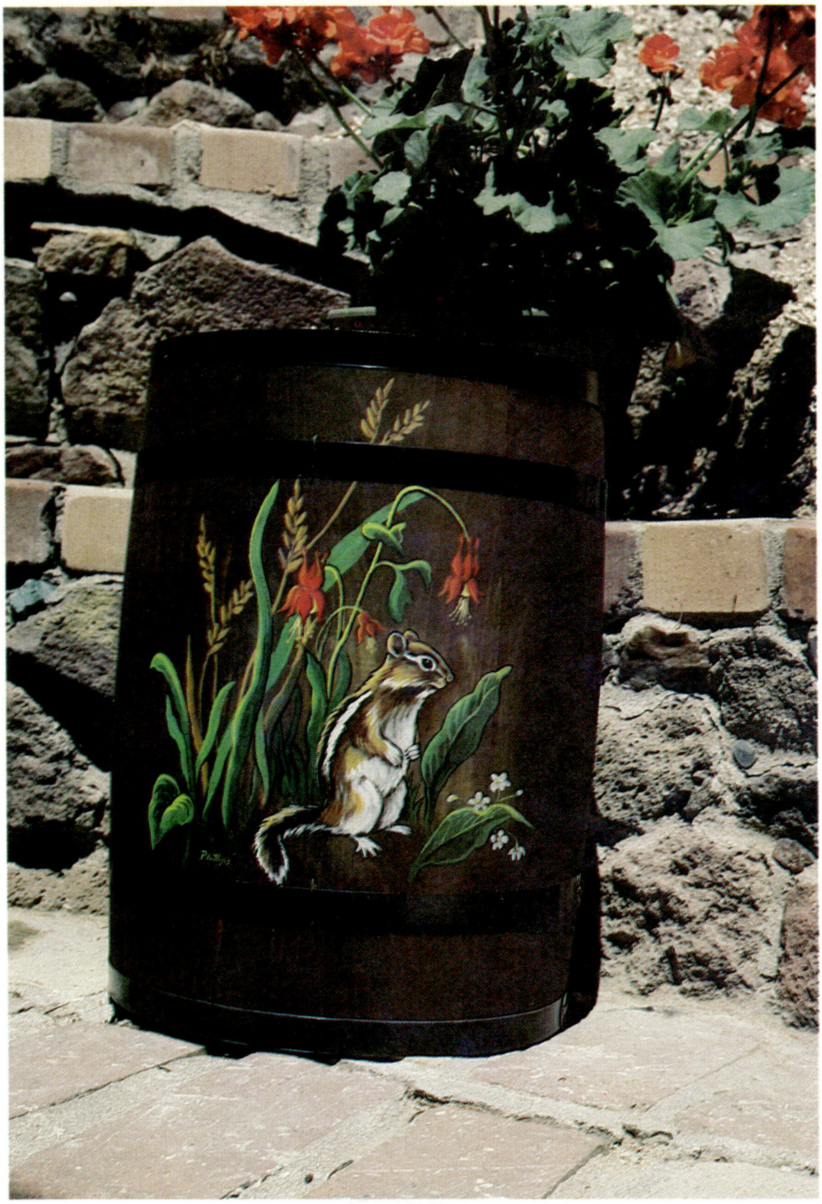

Wooden Barrel with Chipmunk and Columbine

Serving Tray with Lupine and Daisies

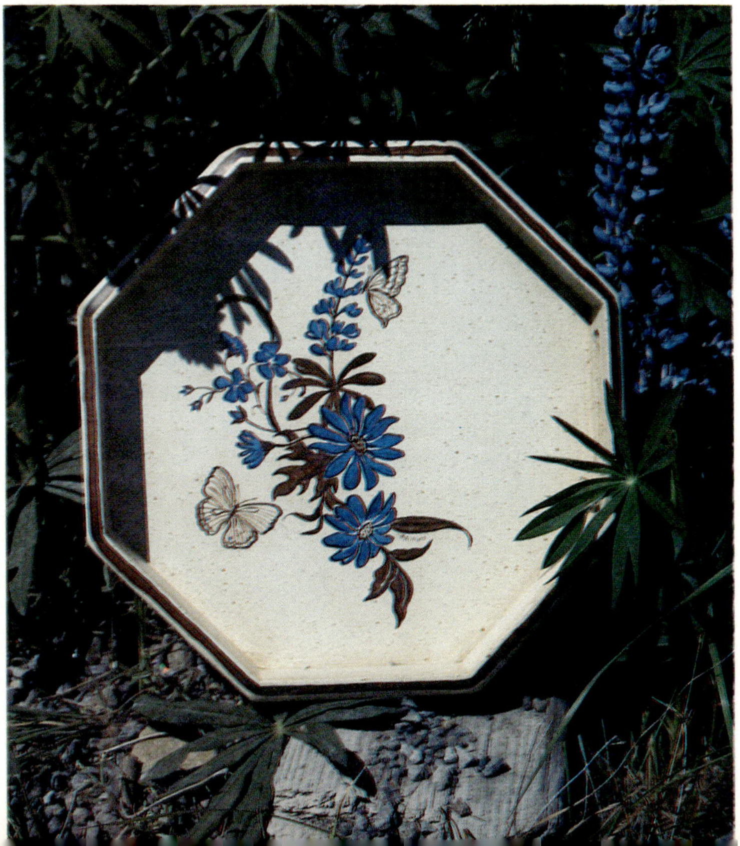

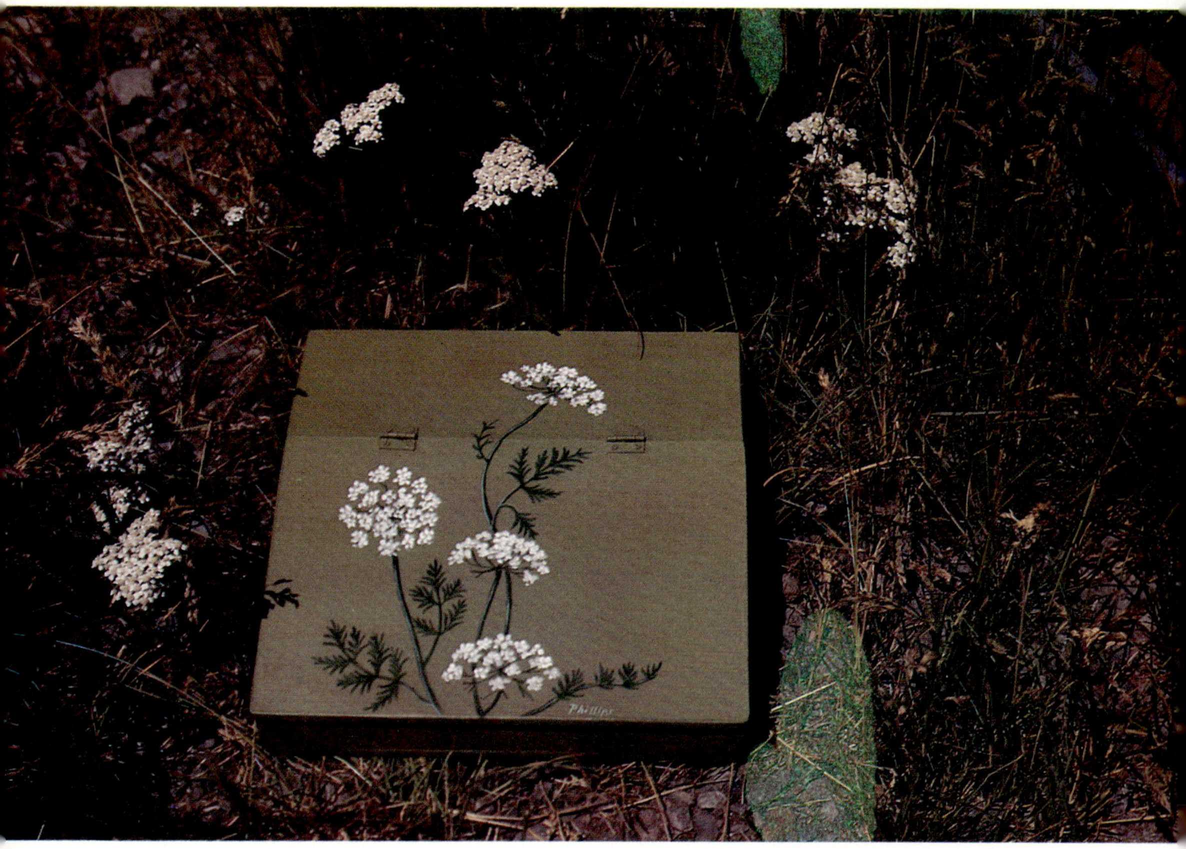

Lap Desk with Queen Anne's Lace

Bobcat on Briefcase

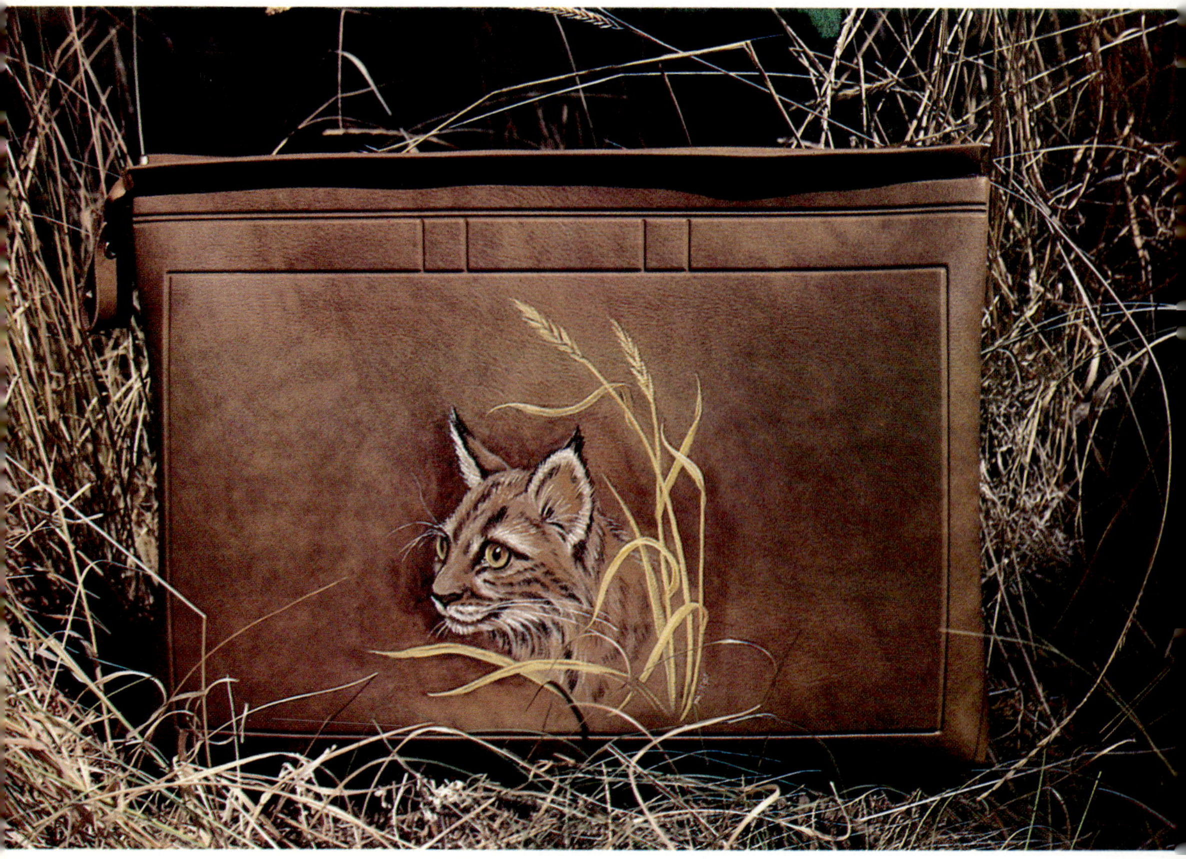

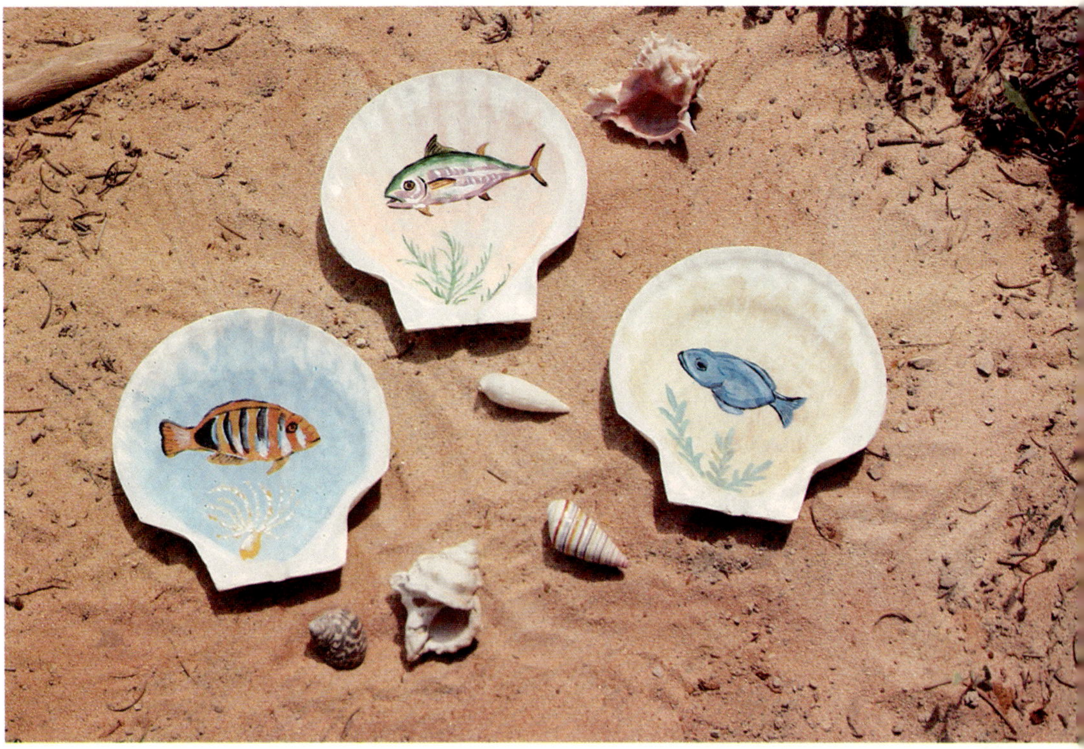

Decorated Shells

Matted Fish Drawing (Designed by Kathy Poulsen)

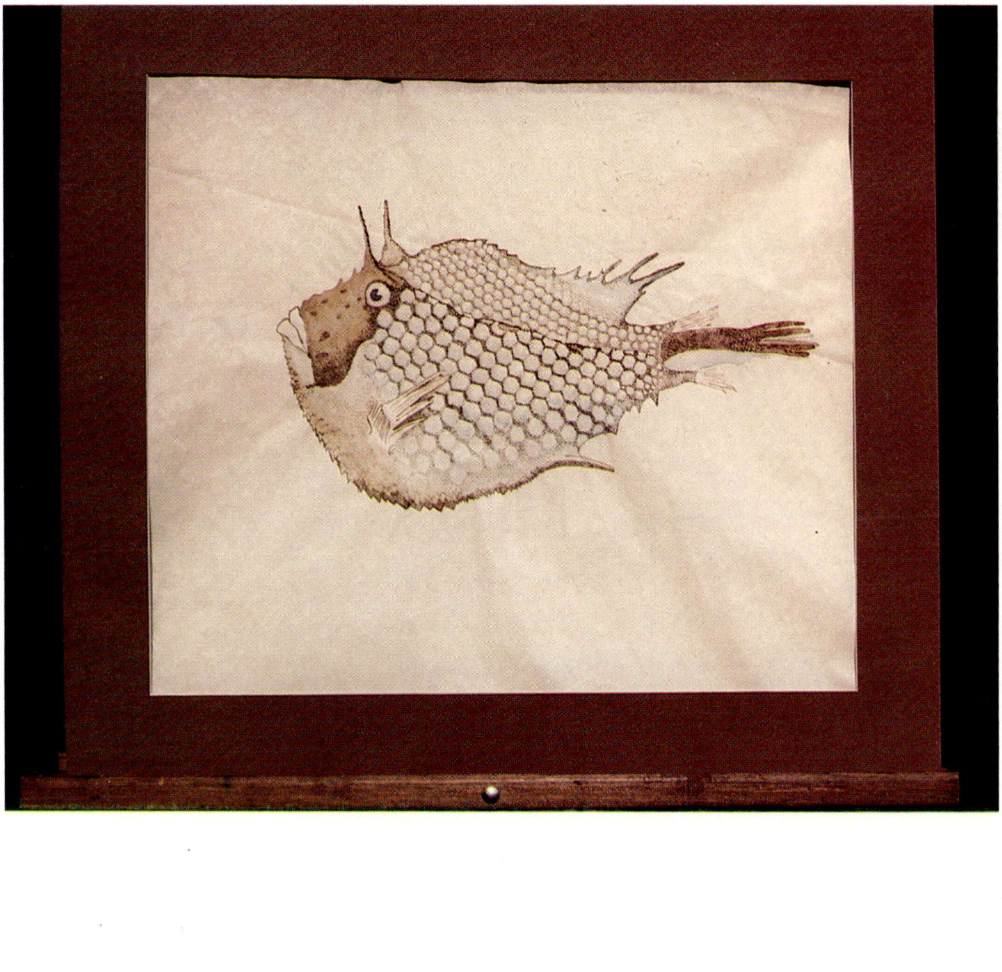

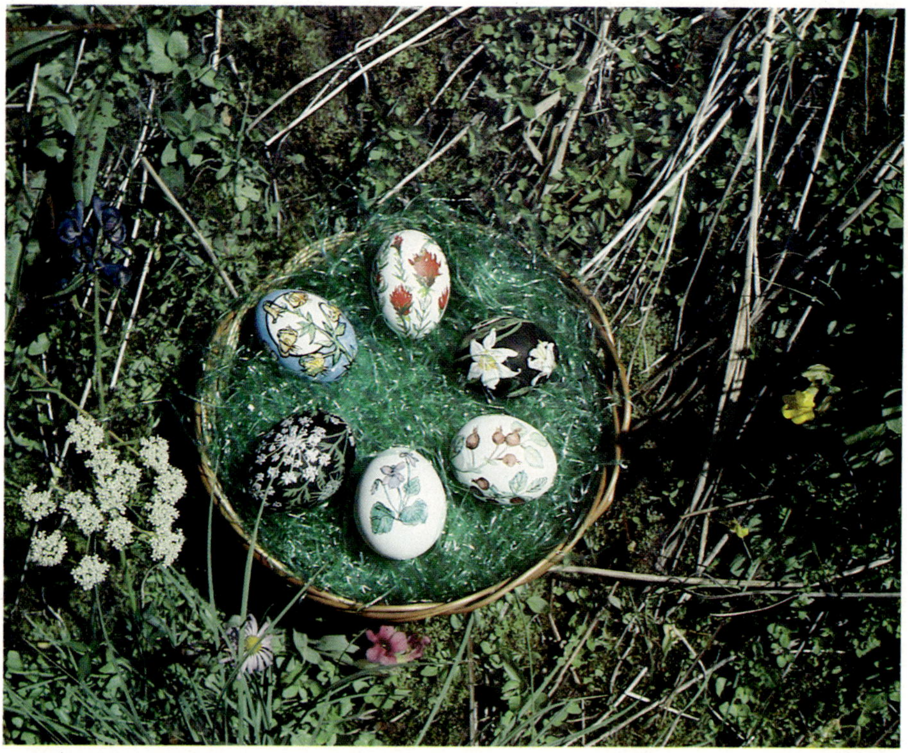

Painted Eggs (Designed by Kathy Poulsen)

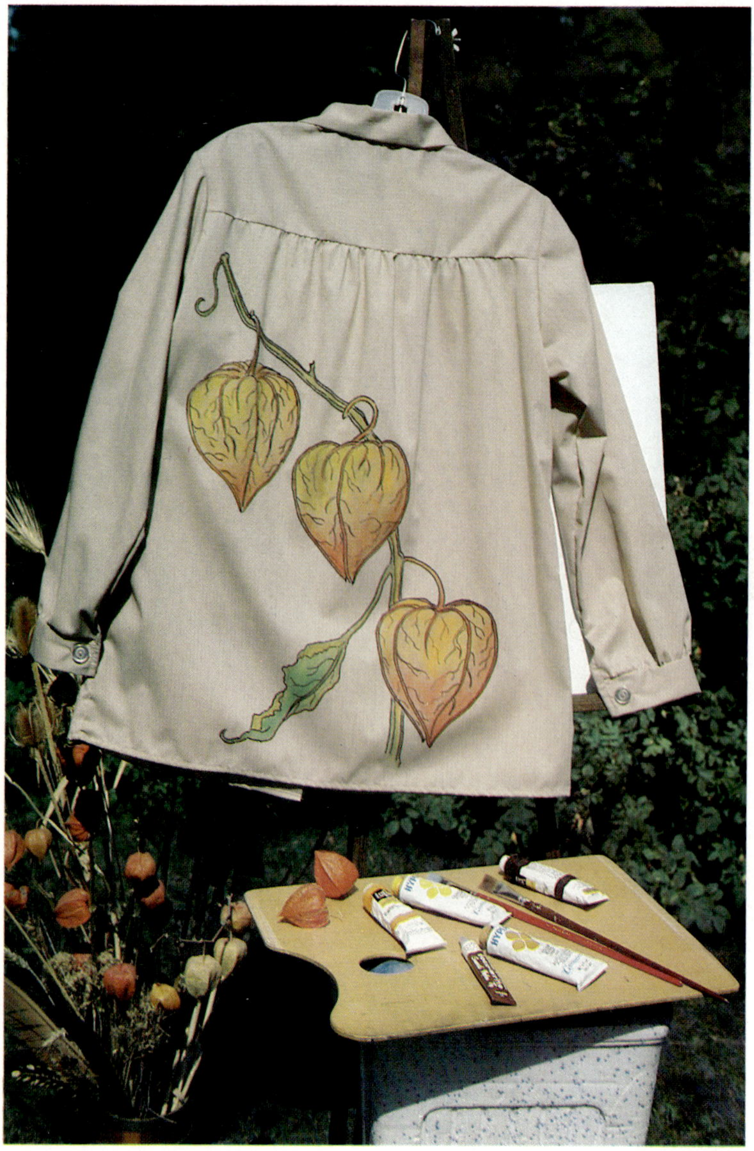

Japanese Lanterns on a Smock

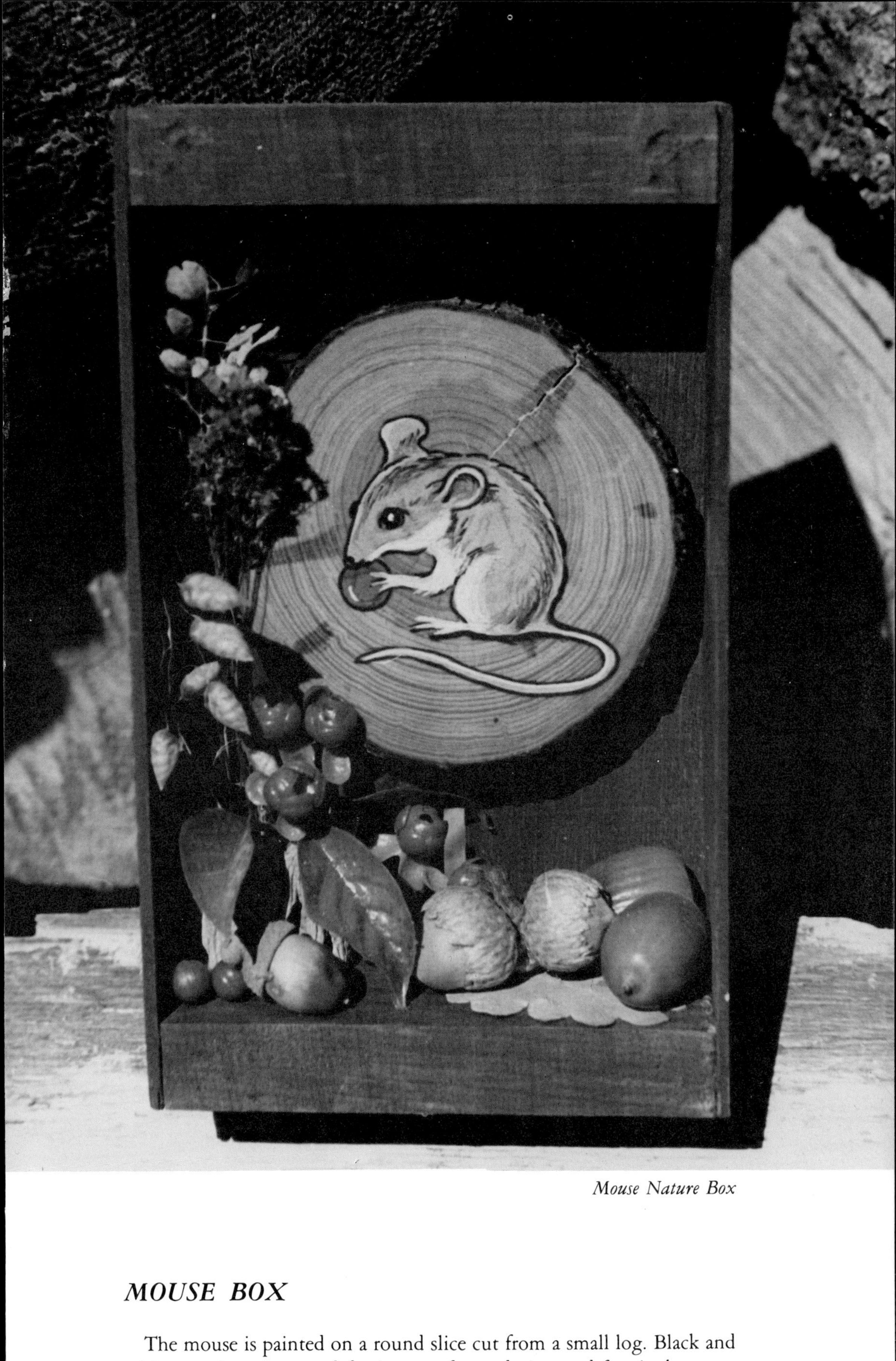

Mouse Nature Box

MOUSE BOX

The mouse is painted on a round slice cut from a small log. Black and white are the colors used for its gray fur; cadmium red for the berry.

Glue it to the inside of a small shadow box. Glue on acorns and nuts, artificial berries, and dried flowers.

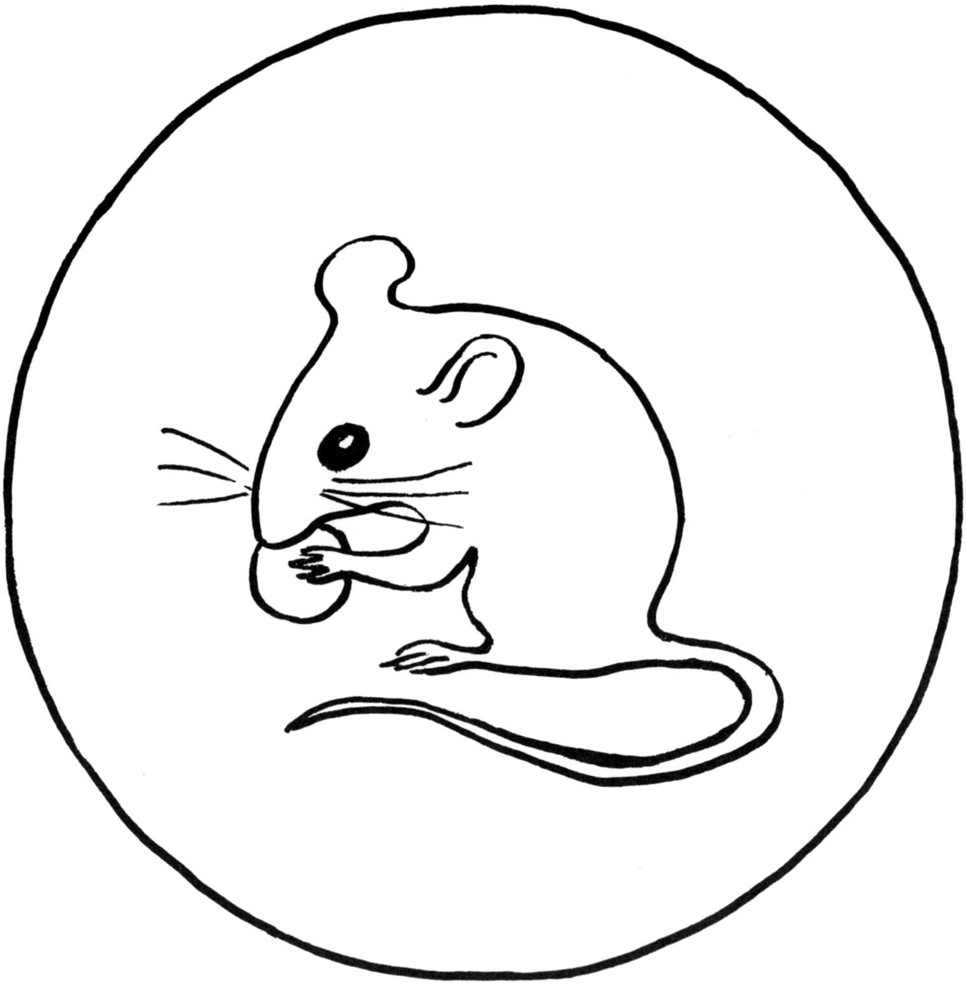

Mouse

SHELLS

These large shells were purchased by the package in the household wares department of a store; their purpose is for serving seafood, but they are useful in other ways.

The smooth inside is painted with a water-thinned wash of pastel color, made by mixing white with acrylic colors. Over this, various designs of fish and seaweeds are added. A glaze of gloss varnish makes the shells durable enough to use as serving dishes.

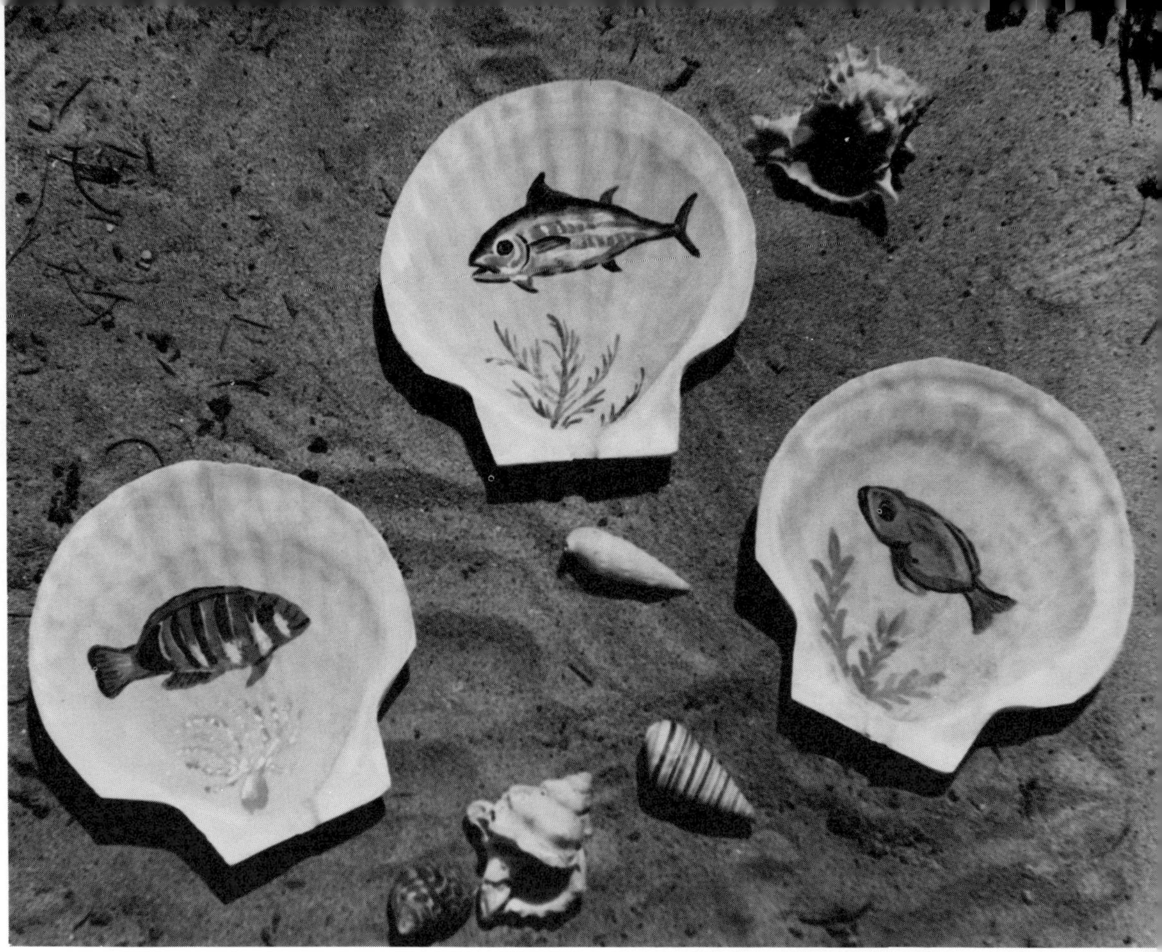

Shells with Acrylic Designs

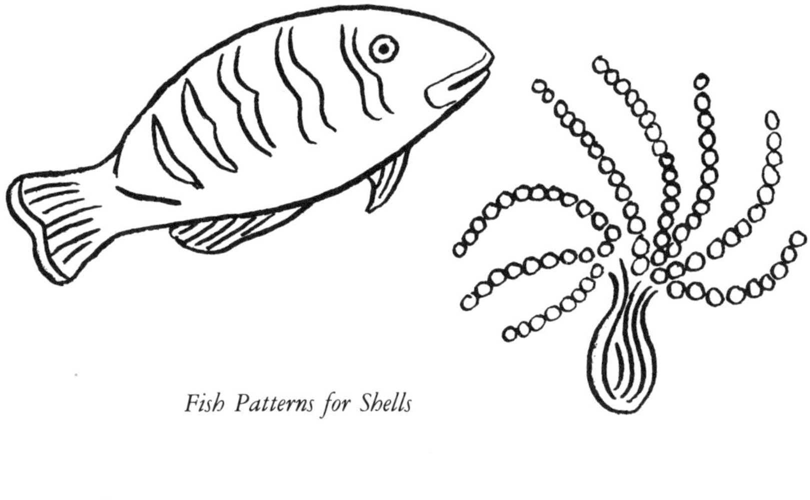

Fish Patterns for Shells

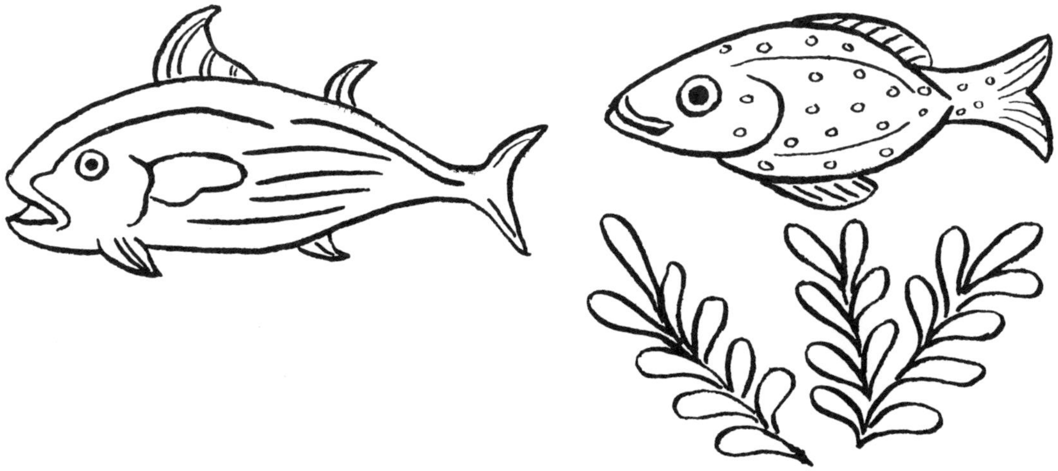

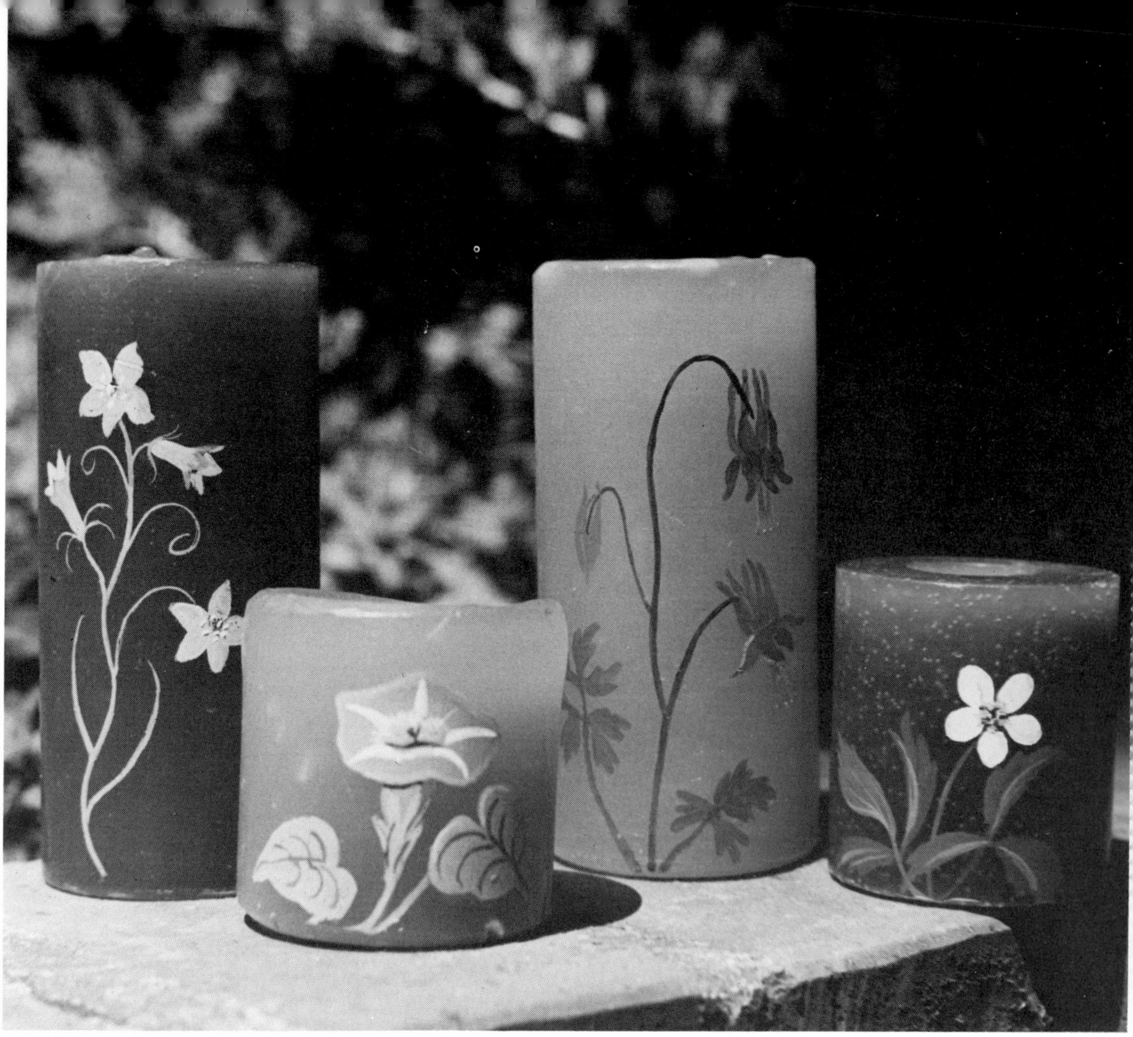

Candles Decorated with Acrylics

CANDLES

Have fun with these. Use candles of all shapes and colors. Paint should be undiluted. Using your pattern for reference, paint on freehand. A mistake can be removed by gently scraping off with your fingernail. Go over the finished design with a gloss varnish for permanence.

GREETING CARDS

Here is a lovely and easy way to use the pressed flower specimens you have been saving.

You will need gloss polymer medium, blank cards (cut and folded of heavy paper stock), white or colored facial tissue (2-ply sheets divided into single sheets), a flat medium-sized brush, and pressed flowers or leaves.

I have used two methods: making the designs directly on the cards or making the designs separately and gluing them onto the cards.

In the first method, paint the area of the card where your design will be with a generous coat of gloss polymer medium. While still wet, carefully place the dried flowers in place. For special effects, glitter or bits of colored tissue can be added at this stage. Over this lay a single ply of facial tissue cut to the correct size. Gently paint with polymer medium, making sure that all areas of the tissue are saturated. It will look milky white but will dry clear. Allow to dry for several hours. Gold trim (paper or fabric) may be glued around the edges as borders.

You may find it easier to make the flower design separately; then cut it to the desired size and glue it onto a blank card. To do this, work on a large sheet of waxed paper so that the design may be peeled away. For the base, use white or colored wrapping tissue or any lightweight paper that is firmer than facial tissue. Cut a size a little larger than what you intend to use, for it will be trimmed down to size. Follow the same procedure as the first method, painting the base tissue with gloss polymer medium, lay the pressed flowers onto a wet surface, place a single ply of tissue over, and coat again with polymer medium. When almost dry, peel carefully from waxed paper. Dry thoroughly. Trim to the correct size and glue to the card. Add a border or mat.

If the dried flowers become faded, brighten them with thin washes of acrylic color, but keep them natural looking.

Greeting Cards from Pressed Flowers

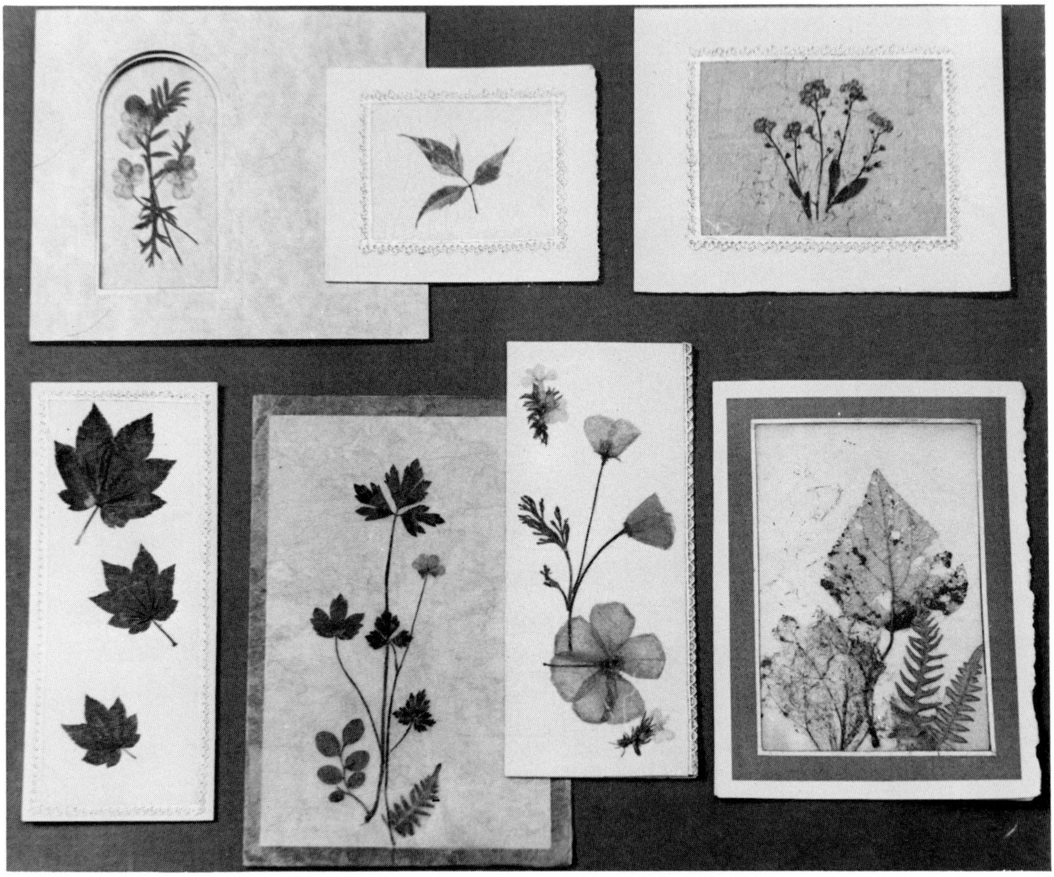

RED FOX

The red fox's fur is a rich red gold, much like the color of the pine box. Therefore, the background around the figure of the fox must be

Red Fox on Cookie Container

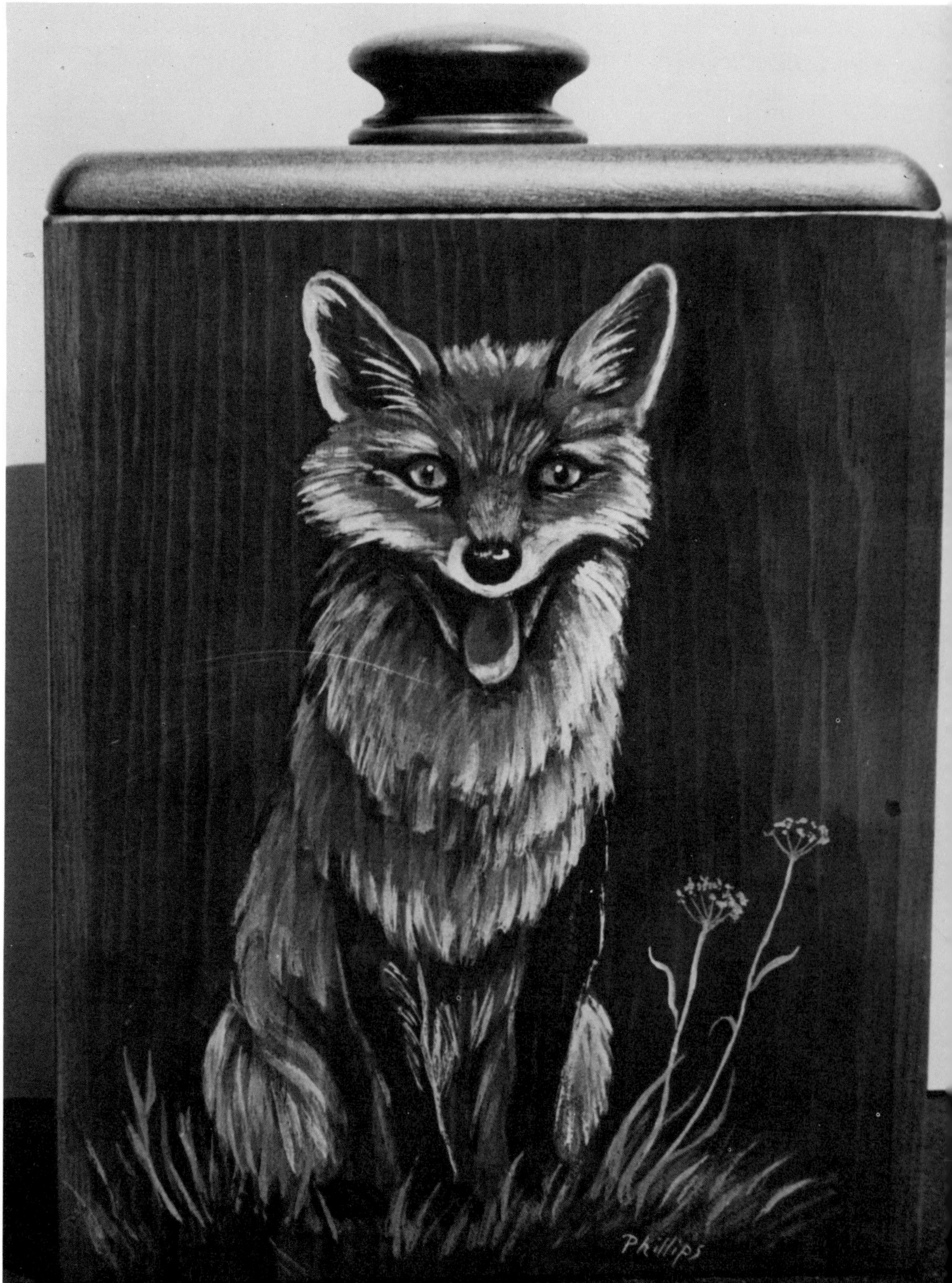

darkened with umber for contrast. Colors used for its fur are burnt sienna and yellow ocher shaded with black and highlighted with white. Brush over the fur with cadmium orange for the reddish glow. Make its eyes luminous with yellow ocher, orange, and white; the pupils black.

Around the sides of the box is a trail of fox tracks painted with yellow ocher. Animal and bird tracks are always decorative and interesting. Try various tracks with your wildlife designs.

Fox Tracks

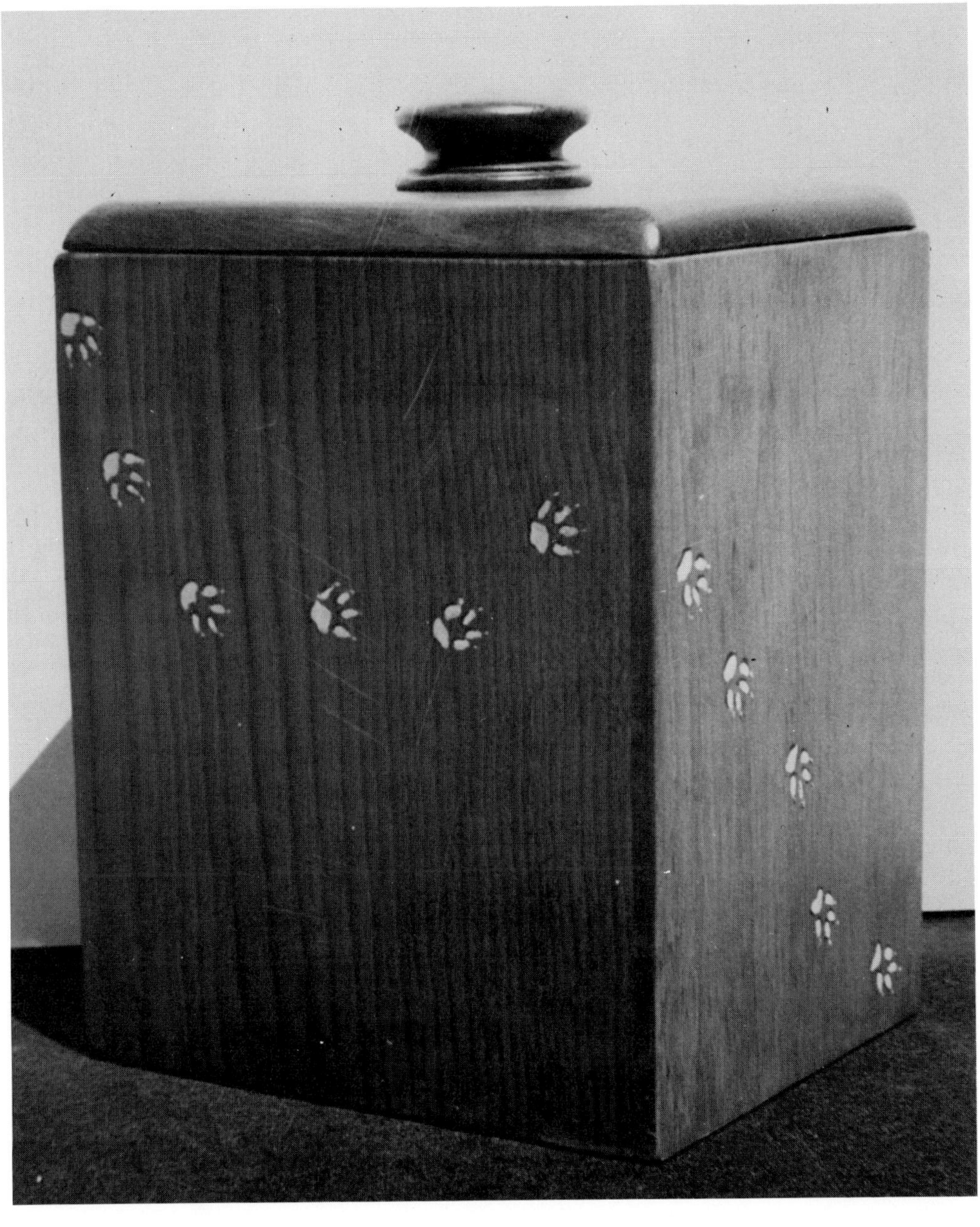

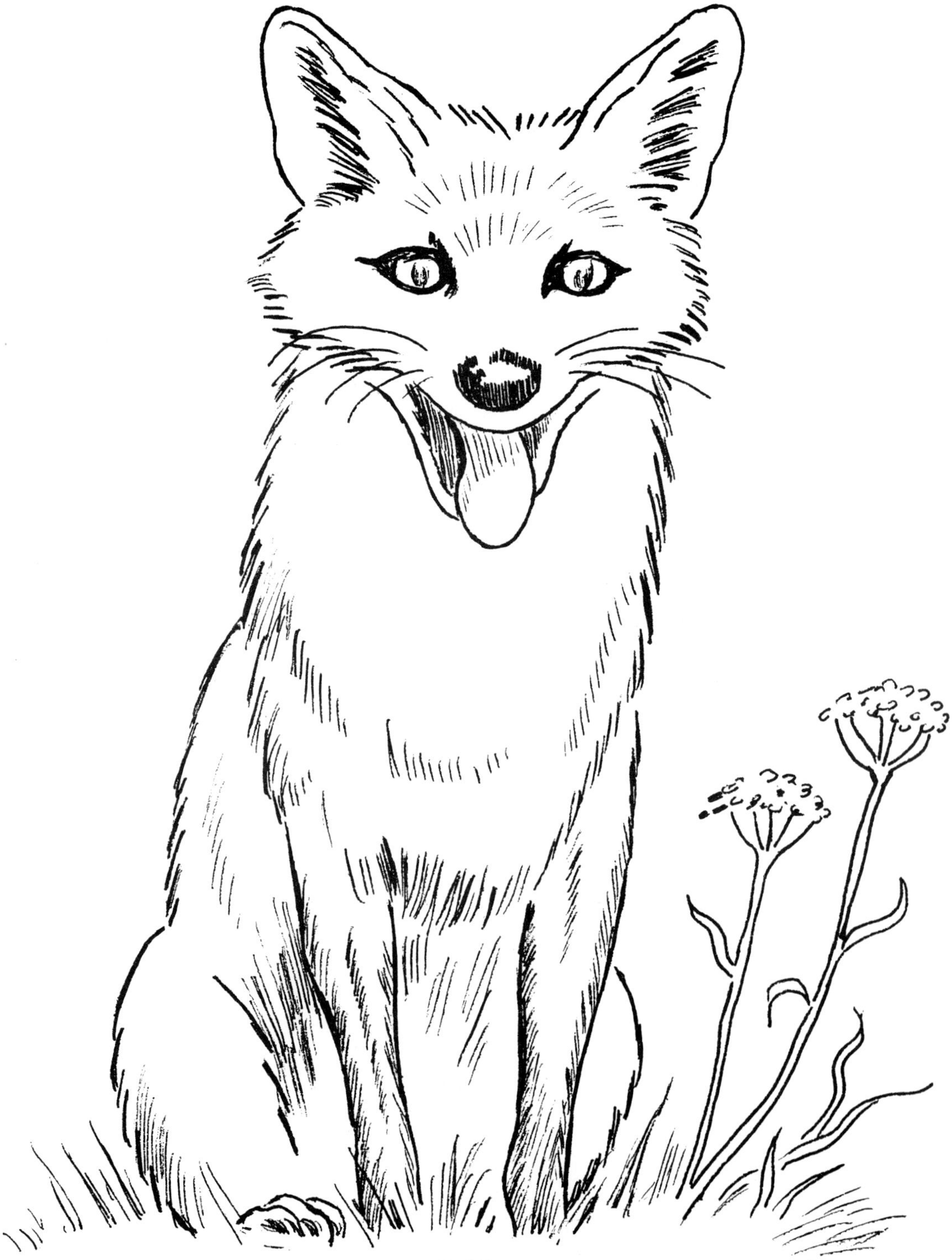

Red Fox

LEAF DESIGNS

The marvelous symmetry of leaves can be incorporated into designs in many ways. Here is a simple use of the leaf form using the actual leaf for a pattern.

Select a single large leaf or a twig of compound leaves. Velveteen-covered pillows are used for this project. Place the leaf in position on the pillow. Hold lightly with fingers and trace around the leaf with a permanent felt marker in the color of your choice. (Brown was used on the orange and cream-colored pillows shown here.)

Remove the leaf and, using it as a guide, draw in the leaf veins with a felt marker.

Leaf Designs on Velveteen Pillows

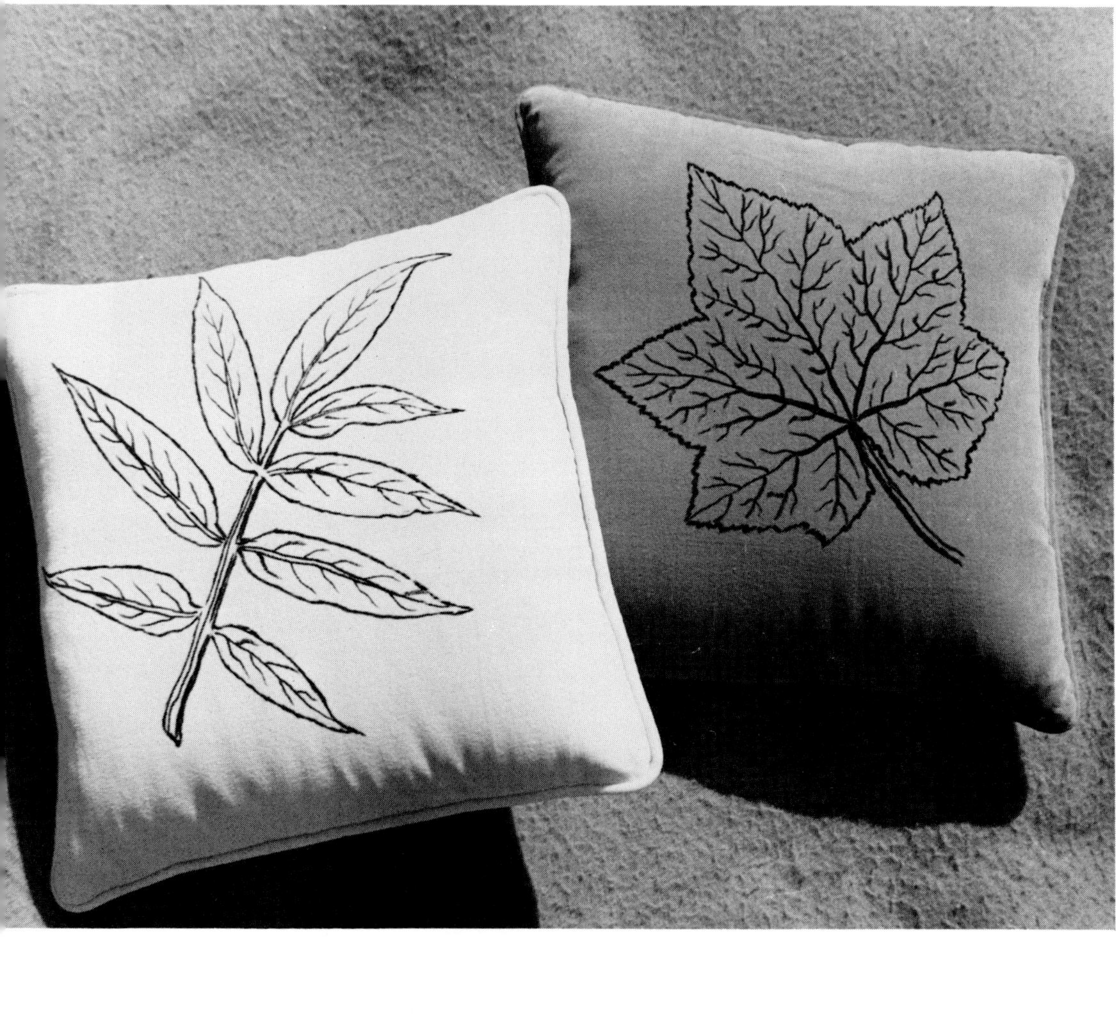

MULE DEER

For an effective winter setting, paint a wooden box a soft shade of gray inside and out by mixing Payne's gray and white. When dry, trace on the pattern. The deer are burnt umber and white. Using a small, flat nylon brush, "sketch" in muscles. Outline with burnt umber. A few simple white areas suggest snow. You may want to varnish the box with gloss polymer medium for extra durability.

Mule Deer on Wooden Box

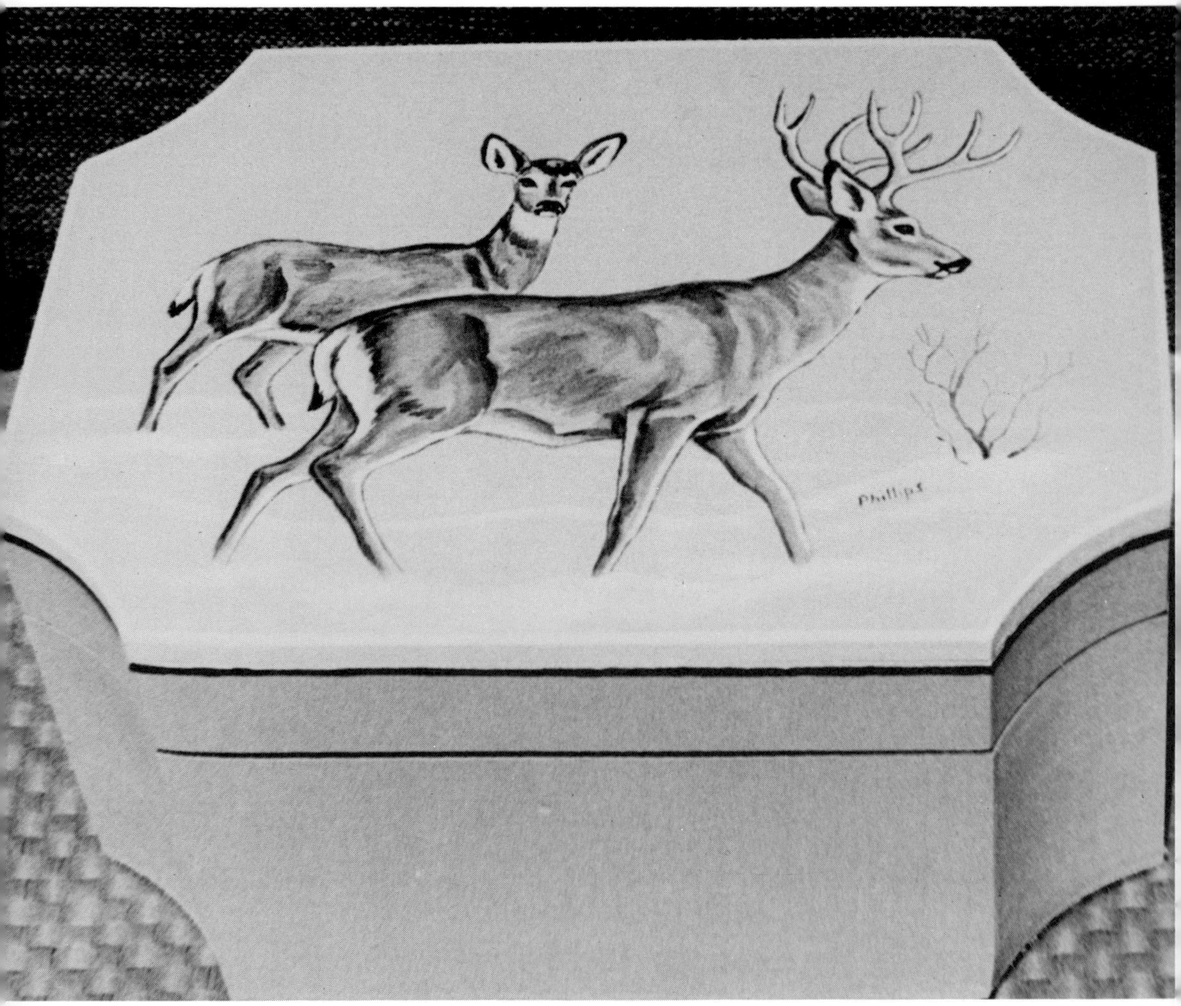

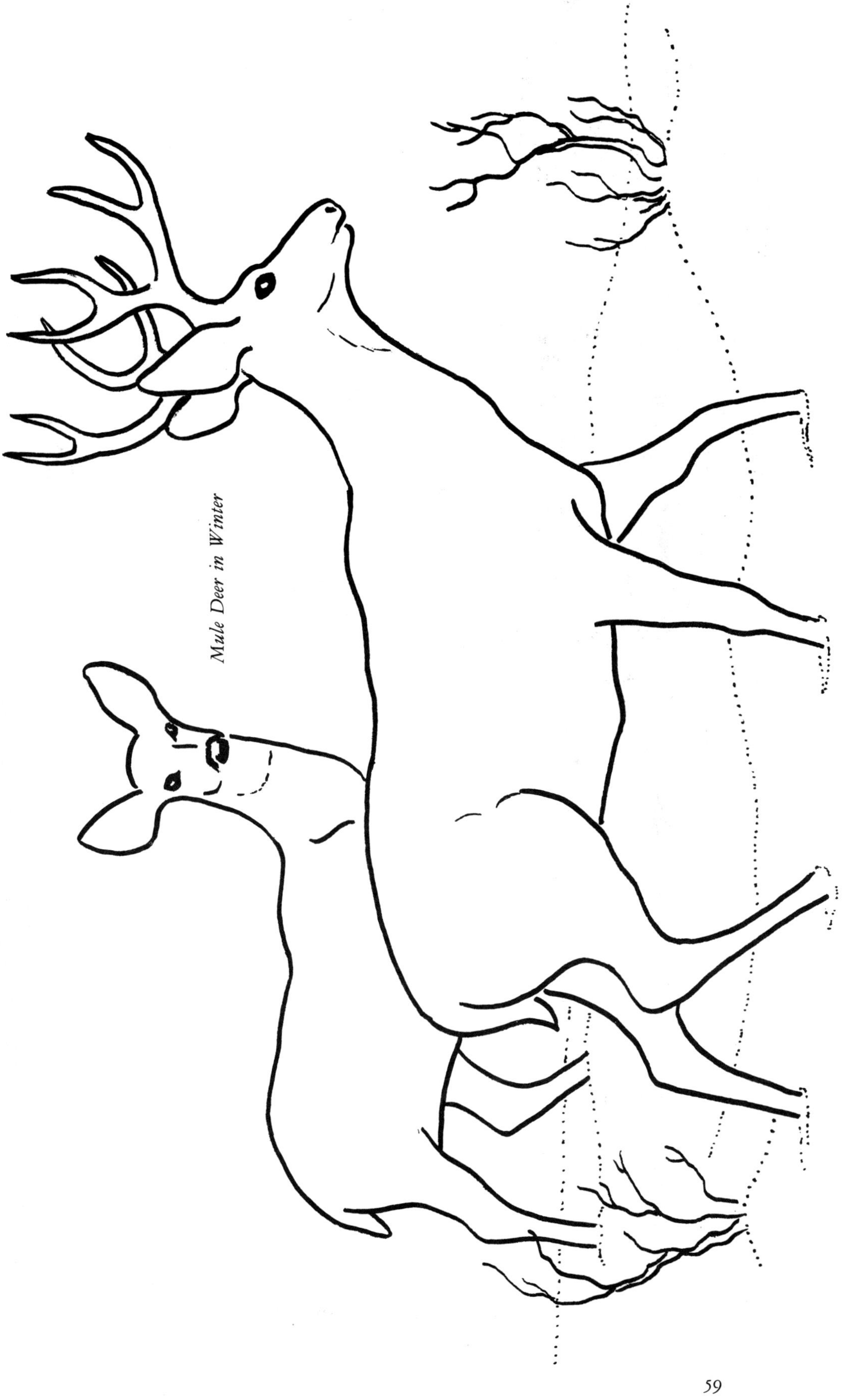

Mule Deer in Winter

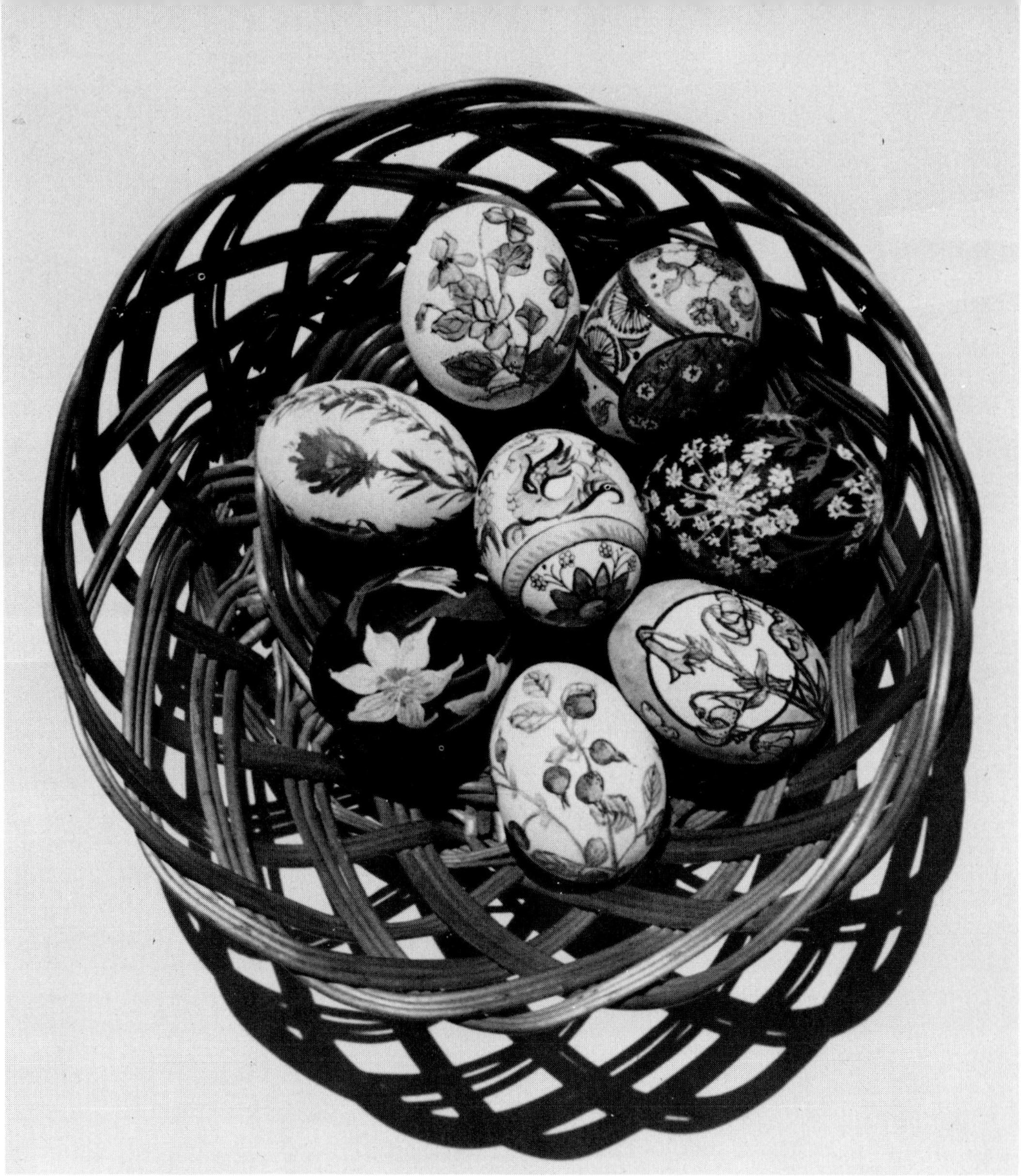

Painted Eggs (Designed by Kathy Poulsen)

EGG PAINTING

To prepare eggs, puncture a small hole in one end with a needle. Make a slightly larger hole in the opposite end. Blowing from the smaller hole, empty the contents of the egg into a dish. Rinse the egg with water and blow again. Dry thoroughly.

Some of the eggs shown were first given a tint of color with acrylic paint. Solid black sets off white designs such as Queen Anne's lace. Other eggs were designed directly on the white shell using a permanent felt-tip pen to draw the flowers. Small designs can be traced on using carbon paper, or draw them freehand. The acrylic paint is thinned to a water-color consistency.

If eggs are to be hung, glue on a loop of thread with white glue. Two coats of gloss polymer medium will give a shiny finish and will help to make the eggshell less fragile.

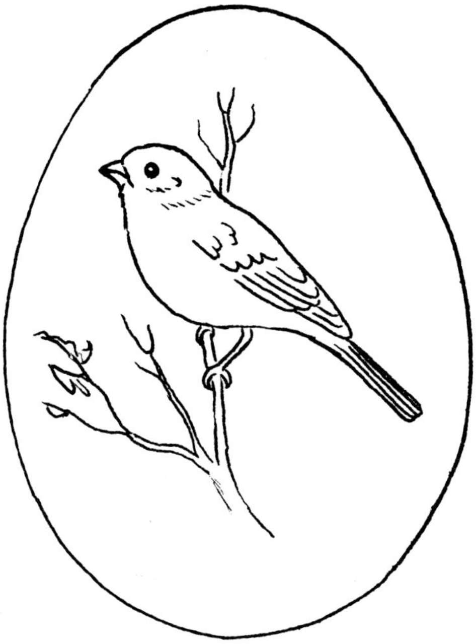
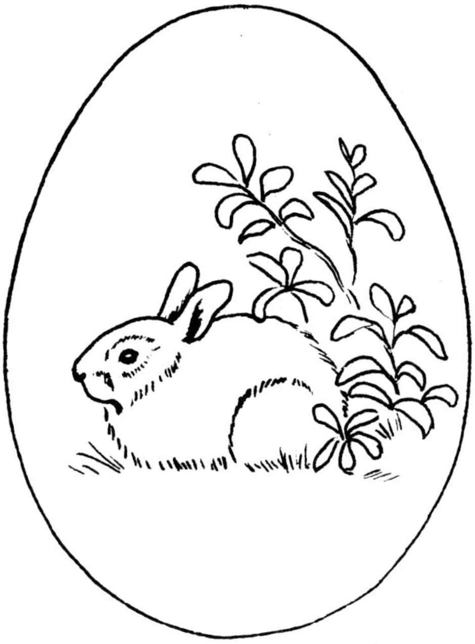

Egg Designs

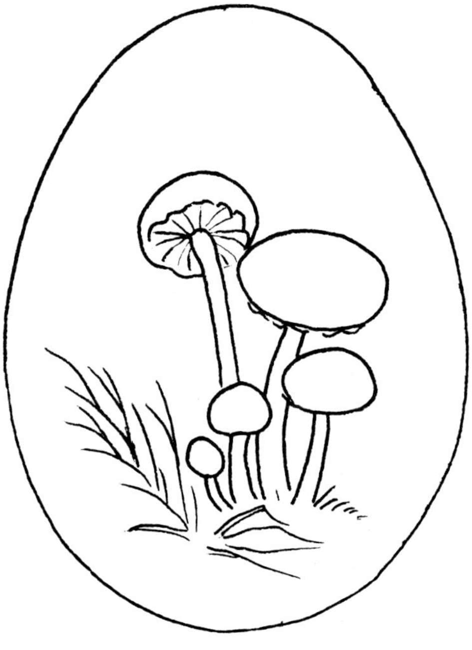
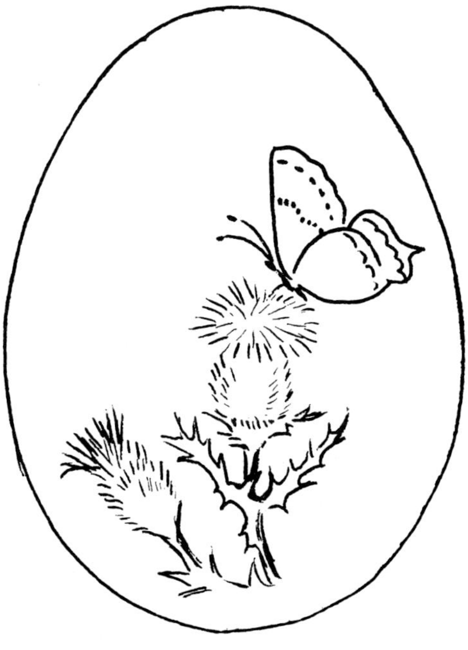

PAINTING ON LEATHER

BOBCAT

There are several kinds of leather; each has different painting qualities. Smooth grained leather will give a different effect than will suede leather. Choose designs best suited for the leather. For example, the bobcat blends well with the tawny, pebbly grain. Suede leather is more difficult to paint on but has a rich, velvety look.

Colors of the bobcat are yellow ocher, black, and white. The natural color of the leather is allowed to show through the design. Burnt umber is rubbed on lightly around the bobcat's head to make it stand out from the background. Grasses are yellow ocher and white.

Too much water added to the acrylic causes it to bead when applied to leather. Keep the paint thick, but apply it sparingly.

Bobcat on Leather Briefcase

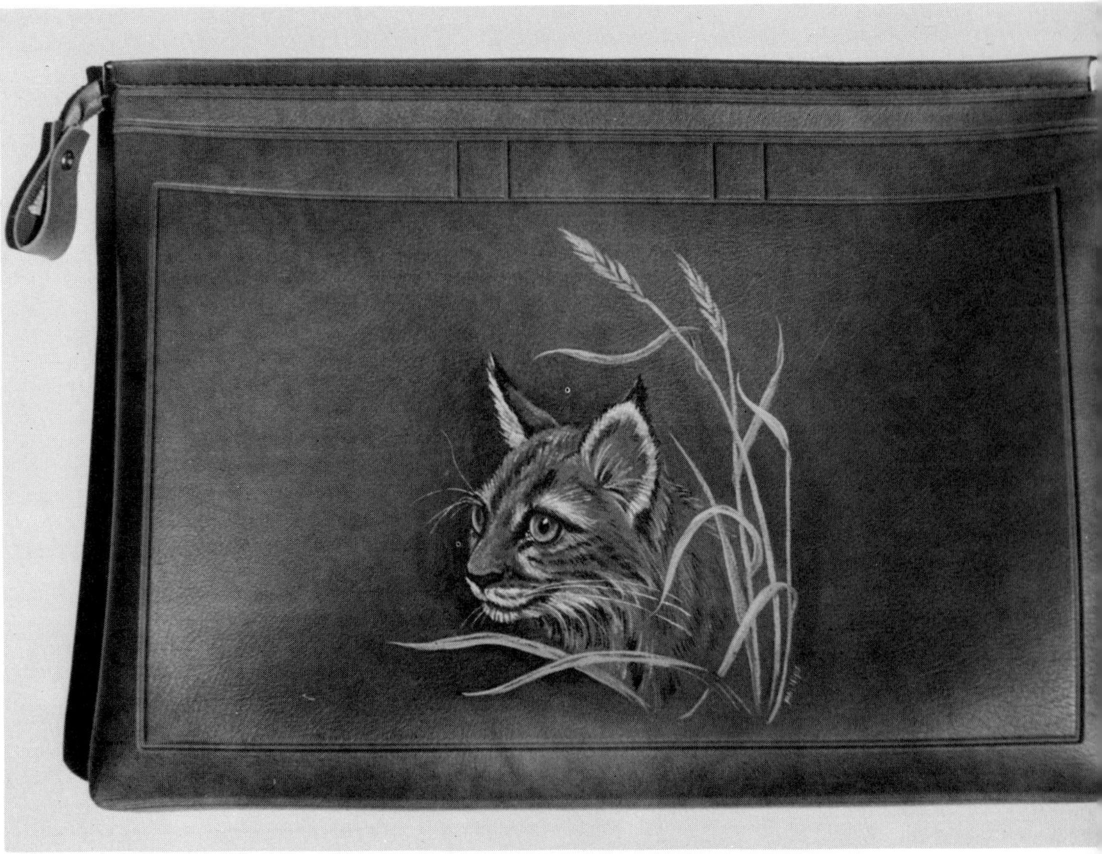

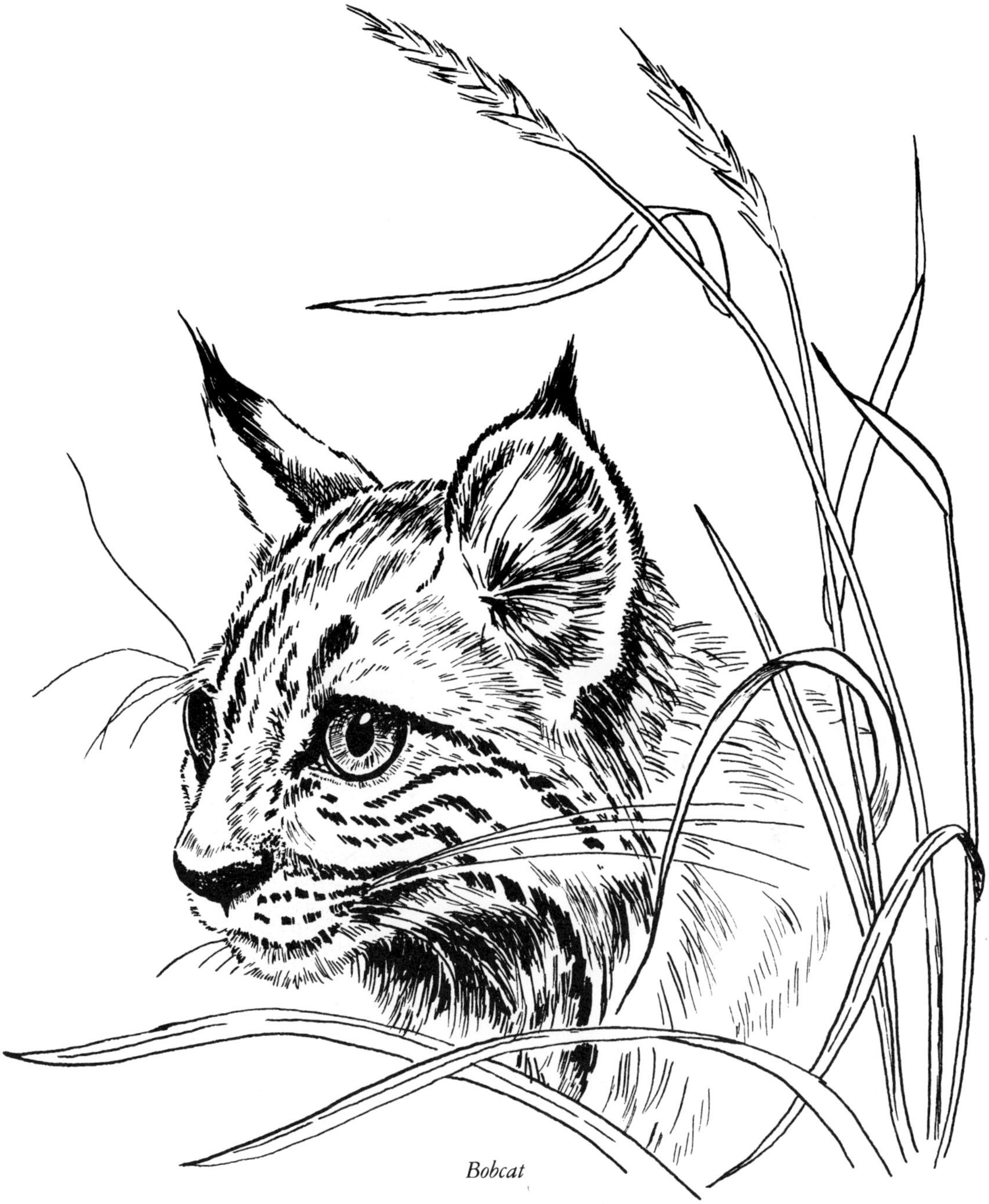

Bobcat

MUSHROOM YARDSTICK HOLDER

The yardstick holder is made from two strips of burlap 6½″ wide by 40″ long. Make a 1″ fringe on the sides of the two strips by pulling threads. On one strip glue on the mushrooms cut from different colors of felt. You may decorate the mushrooms before gluing by painting with acrylic, with a permanent felt marker, or by sewing on seed beads. Add a few blades of grass cut from felt or chain stitched with yarn.

Put the two strips together with the wrong side out and stitch a 1″ seam across the bottom. Turn right side out. Fold under top seam 1″. Stitch the strips together along two sides close to the fringe. Sew a ring to the top of the outside strip for hanging.

To add a decorative tassel, cut with pinking shears a piece of felt 5″ by 6″. On each side make cuts 2″ in length spaced ½″ apart. Fold in half along uncut center. Roll up and add a few stitches to hold tassel together at the top. Attach to the bottom of the holder.

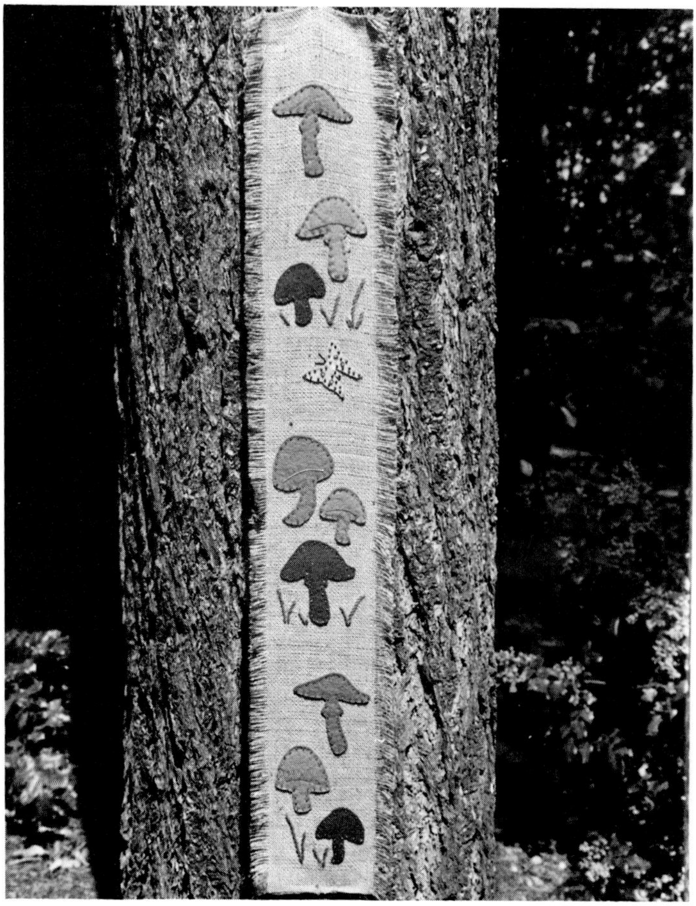

Mushroom Yardstick Holder (Designed by Mary Matlack)

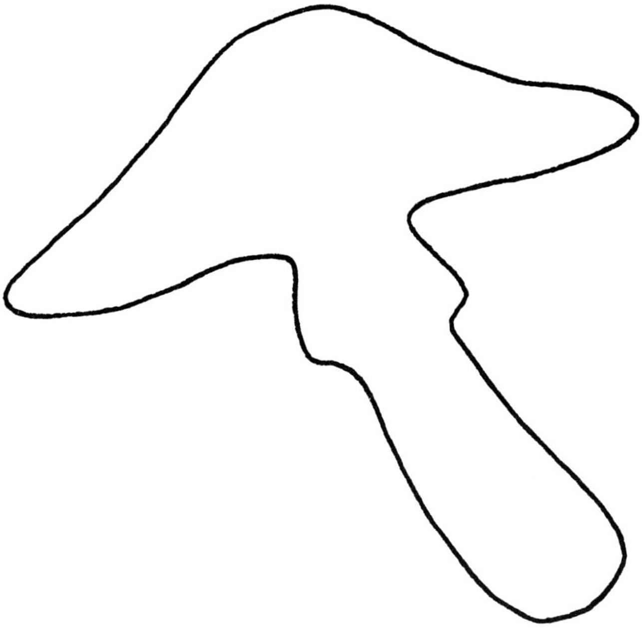

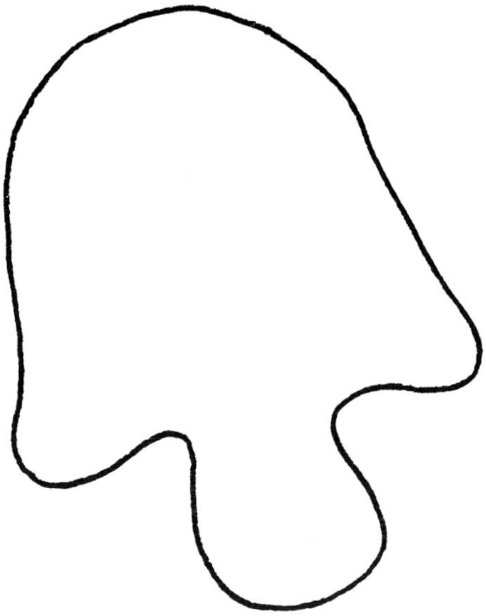

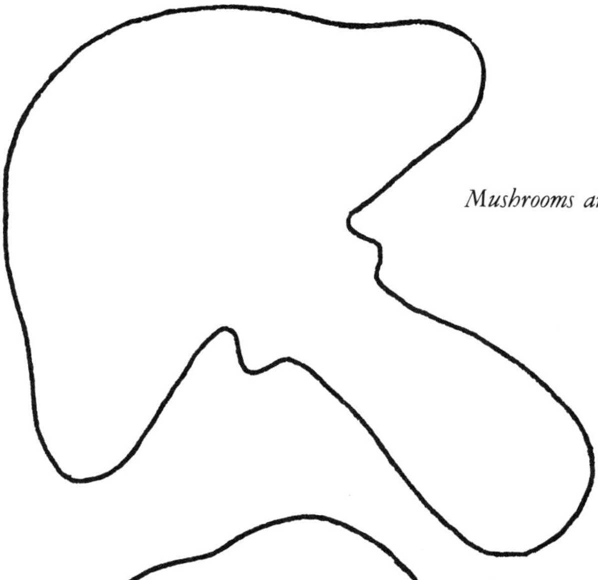

Mushrooms and Yardstick Holder Diagram

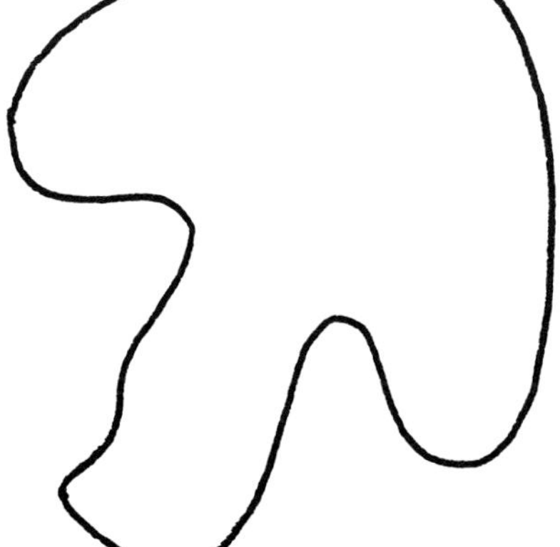

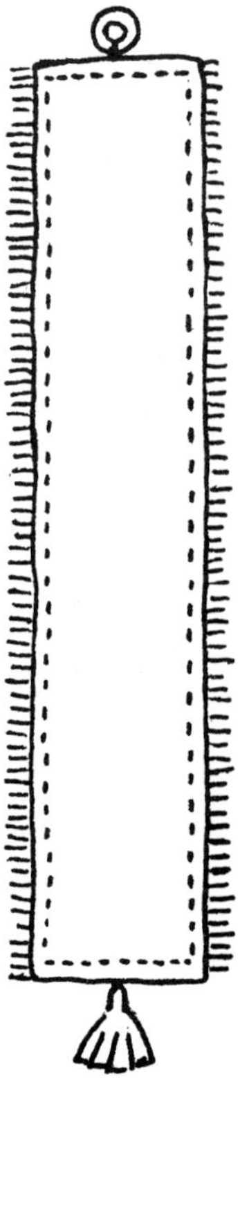

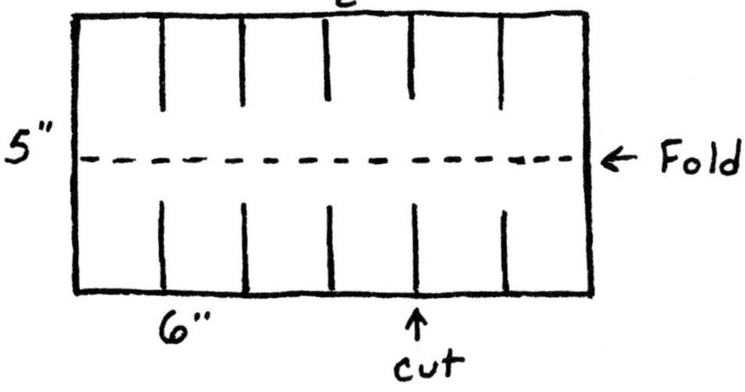

MUSHROOM PRINTING

You can decorate with mushroom prints by using the actual vegetable. Slice a mushroom in half from cap to stem. Paint the cut surface evenly with acrylic paint and press onto paper. For variation, try dabbing several shades of color on the mushroom and printing. Use different sizes of mushrooms.

The prints can be made on greeting cards, wrapping paper, stationery with matching envelopes, or on fabric.

Other vegetables can be used for printing as well, such as apple, onion, cucumber, artichoke.

For an interesting wood grain background, use a piece of soft wood that has been rubbed with steel wool to raise the grain. Give the wood a coat of paint. Working quickly before the paint dries, press paper over the wood and rub with your palm. Use a light-colored paint for the background and print the mushroom design in a darker paint.

Mushroom Printed Stationery

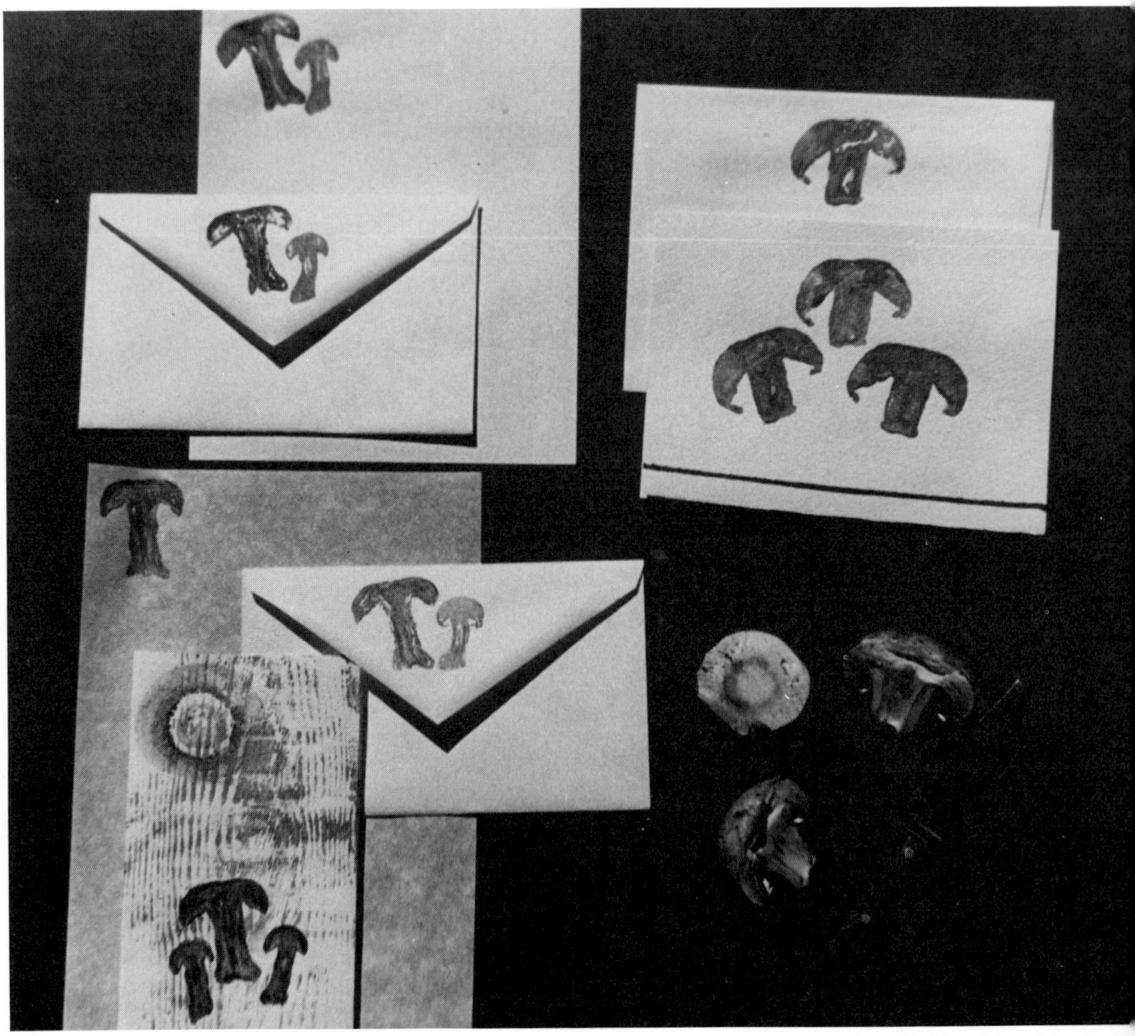

7
Macro-Designs

Macro-drawing is enlarging a small object many times its actual size. It is a good way to sharpen your awareness of the beauty around us that is often hidden and so, unobserved.

Here is how to make macro-designs:

1. Select a specimen with interesting features; a flower, dandelion seed head, thistle, or dried teasel are some subjects you may want to try. (It may be easier for you to begin by using a good enlarged photograph to draw from; thus, you won't be faced with the problem of interpreting three-dimension in your drawing.)

2. Examine the object closely, using a magnifying glass if necessary. Discover its structural pattern.

3. Using a soft pencil, draw an enlarged outline of your object keeping proportions as accurate as possible. Next draw those details that contribute to the overall design.

4. Go over your pencil lines with ink for your final drawing. For interest try using dots in a stippling manner instead of solid lines. You can make your enlarged designs dramatic with strong highlights and deep shadows. Have the source of light come from one direction only. You may wish to transfer your drawing to a piece of tracing paper and apply it to an object as a design.

JAPANESE LANTERNS

To paint a macro-design on a garment (such as the smock pictured here) use acrylic paint and a ball-point tube of fabric paint for drawing the lines. Work out the outlines of your design on a large sheet of wrapping paper, or work it in segments if the design is very large. Go over the lines with black ink. If the material of the garment is lightweight Dacron, it will be possible to place the pattern beneath it and trace it through with a pencil.

Place newspapers or paper towels beneath the garment because the paint will go through the fabric. With the tube of fabric paint (brown

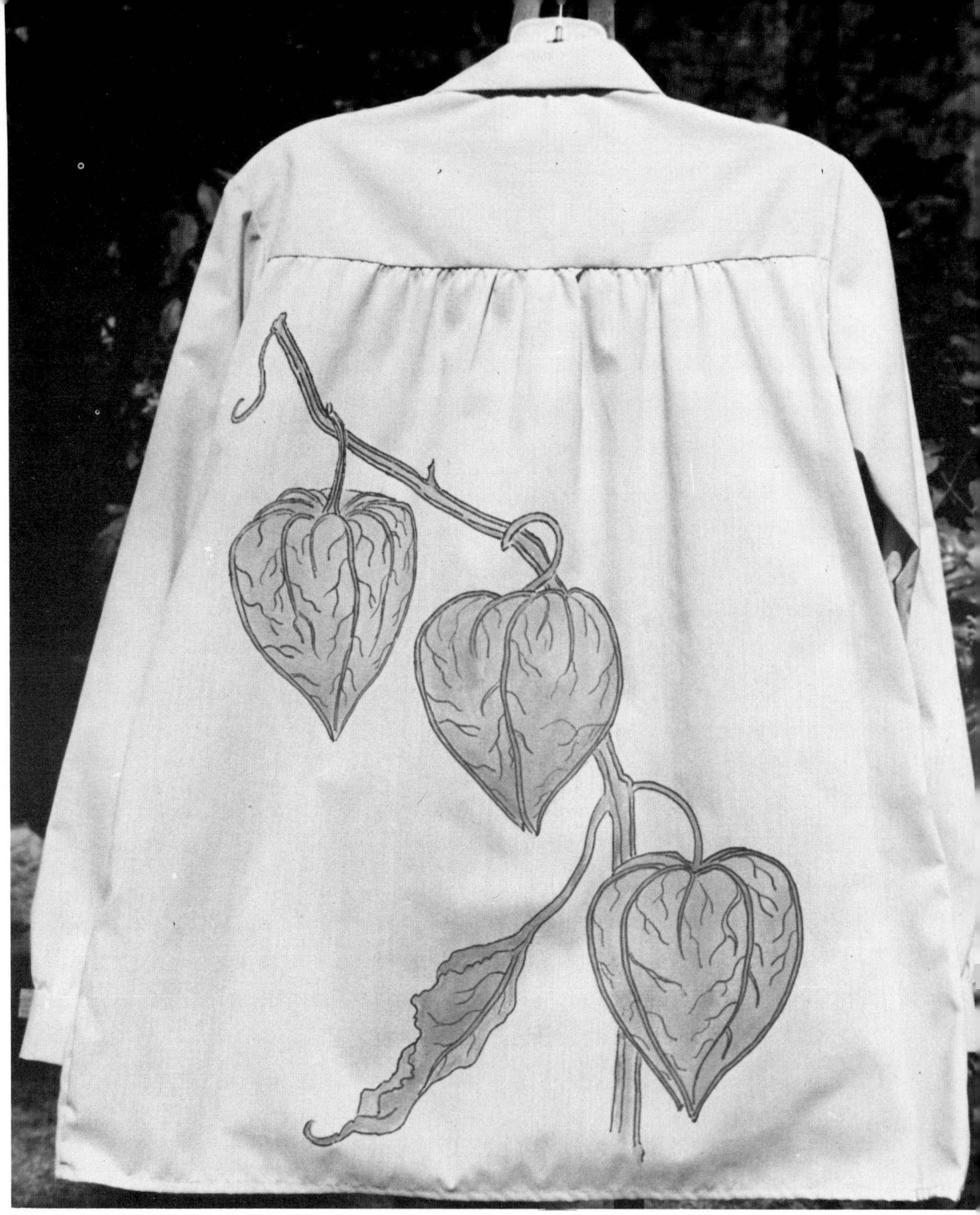

Macro-Design of Japanese Lanterns on a Smock

was used on the Japanese lanterns) draw over the pencil outline. Next fill in detail lines. Allow to dry.

With a wad of paper towel wrapped over your finger, dip in water-thinned paint and brush the color over the design. Do not try to brush right to the edge of the design; this can be finished later with a paintbrush.

The Japanese lanterns are shaded from light at the top to darker points with the following colors: medium cadmium yellow, yellow ocher, cadmium orange, and cadmium red light. The stems are yellow ocher mixed with a touch of green. Add more green for the leaf.

After the paint has dried, press with a warm iron to help set the colors.

Macro-drawing: Japanese Lantern

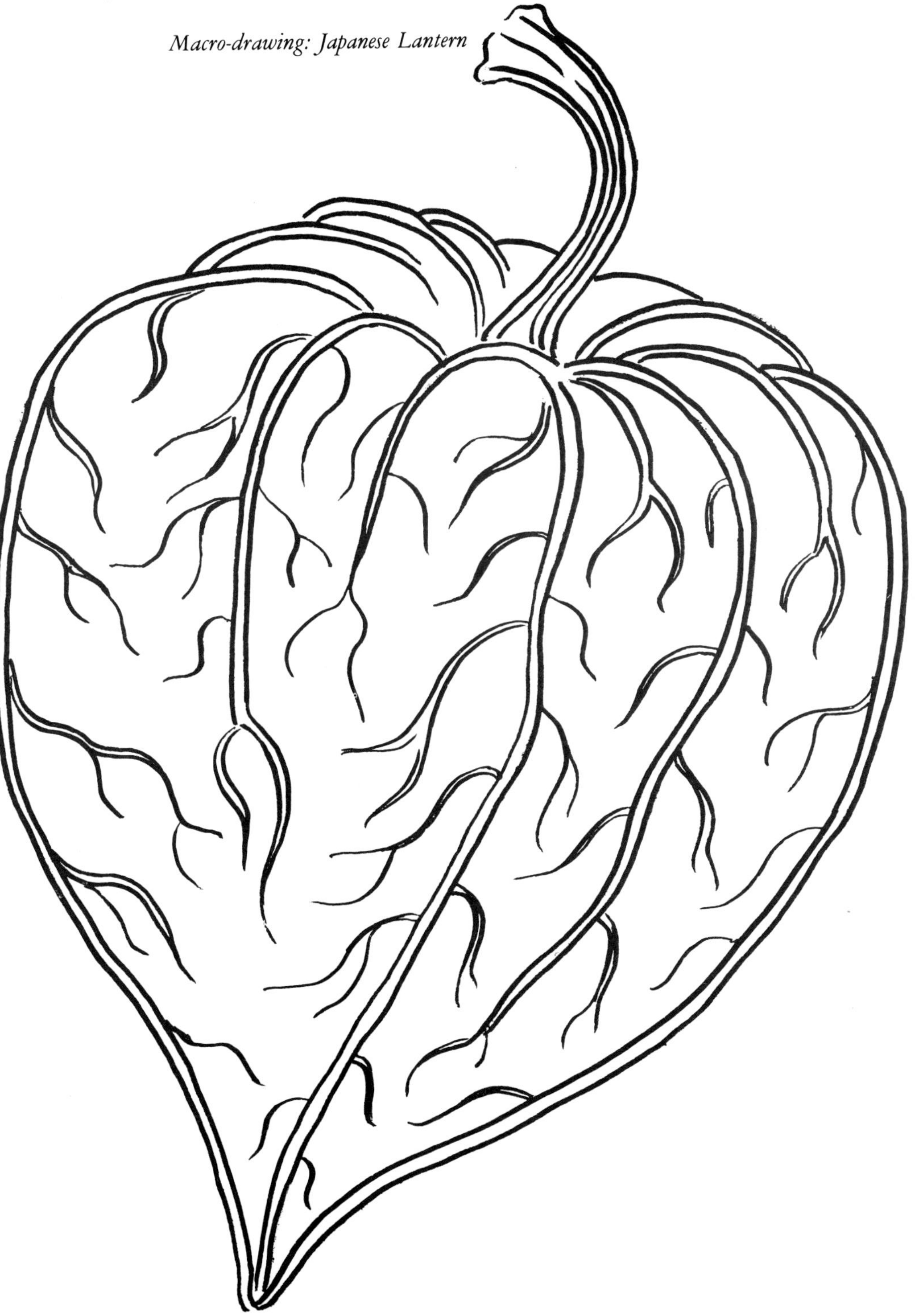

THISTLE WALL HANGING

Macro-designs make dramatic wall hangings. This one is drawn on a medium-weight lining material called Pellon that can be purchased in a fabric store. It is a smooth material on which paint glides freely with no blurring on the edges. Since it is fairly transparent you may place your sketch beneath it and trace over it with a pencil. Then go over all the lines with a permanent felt- or nylon-tip marker. Make sure the marking pen is truly permanent or it will smear when painted over with acrylics.

Acrylic paints are quite thinned with water. The thistle head is violet and white; the stickers are cadmium yellow medium and permanent green light. The rest of the thistle is painted permanent green.

When the painting is dry, cut a second piece of lining the same size and glue together along the top and bottom for extra opaqueness.

The top and bottom are framed with two strips of square doweling cut to the size of the drawing. The strips are painted permanent green, and thin velvet green ribbon is glued to the tops of the sticks. The doweling is glued to the edges of the drawing with white glue.

Attach a small plaque hanger to the back of the top doweling or tack on a length of green velvet ribbon for hanging.

Macro-Design of Thistle on a Wall Hanging

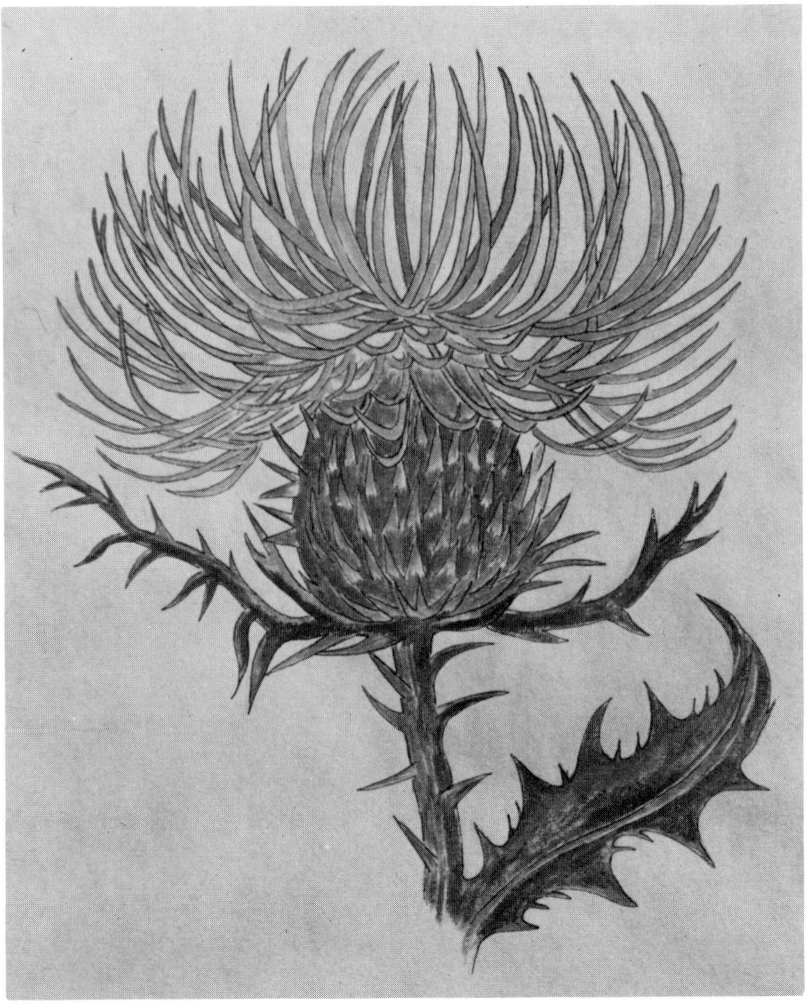

SEED HEAD OF SALSIFY

The fluffy seed head of the salsify (sometimes called goatsbeard) is much like a dandelion seed head. To use one as a model for your macrodesign, carefully pick a newly formed head and spray with hair spray; otherwise the seeds will blow away in the slightest breeze.

If the pattern of seeds seems too intricate, pluck out the top half of the seeds so that you are looking at a cross section. Place on a darker background so the design stands out. A large, round salad bowl will set off the design nicely.

Using white with a little yellow ocher added, paint the stems. Add the seeds with white paint and a fine pointed brush. Keep your design as symmetrical as you can.

If the designed item is going to be used, such as a salad bowl, spray with a clear acrylic varnish.

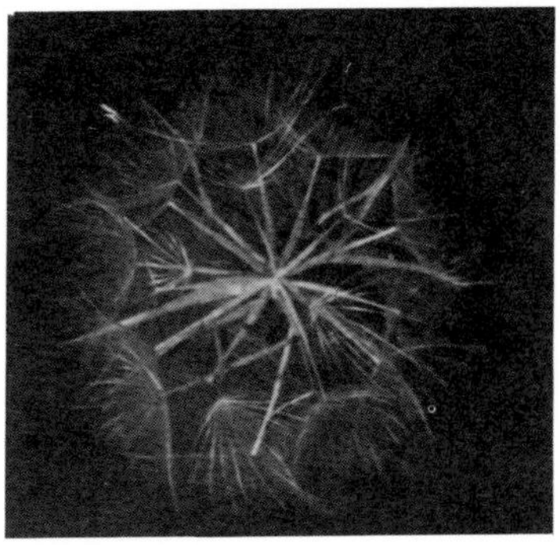

Seed Head of Salsify on a Salad Bowl

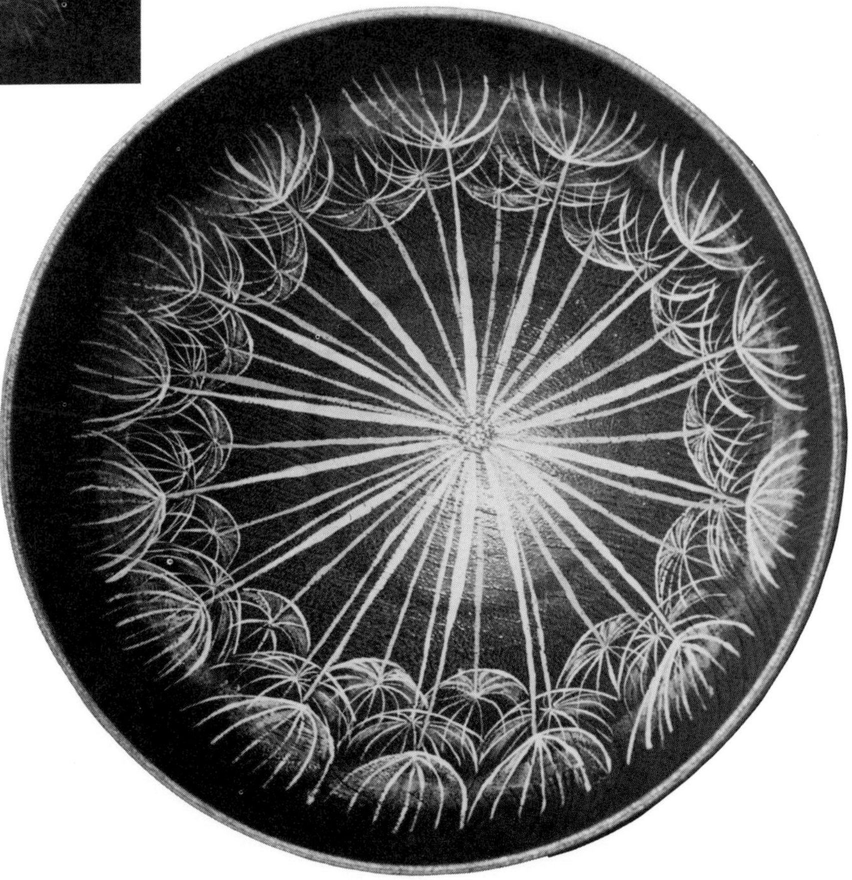

FISH DESIGNS

Much time and effort has been put into your drawings. They should be proudly displayed or put to use in your home.

You may cut a mat from white or colored mat board. If you cut the outside edges to a standard size (16″ by 20″, 18″ by 24″, etc.), you may find a ready-made frame to fit; or fasten the drawing to the mat with masking tape and hang without framing.

Fish Drawing Matted (Designed by Kathy Poulsen)

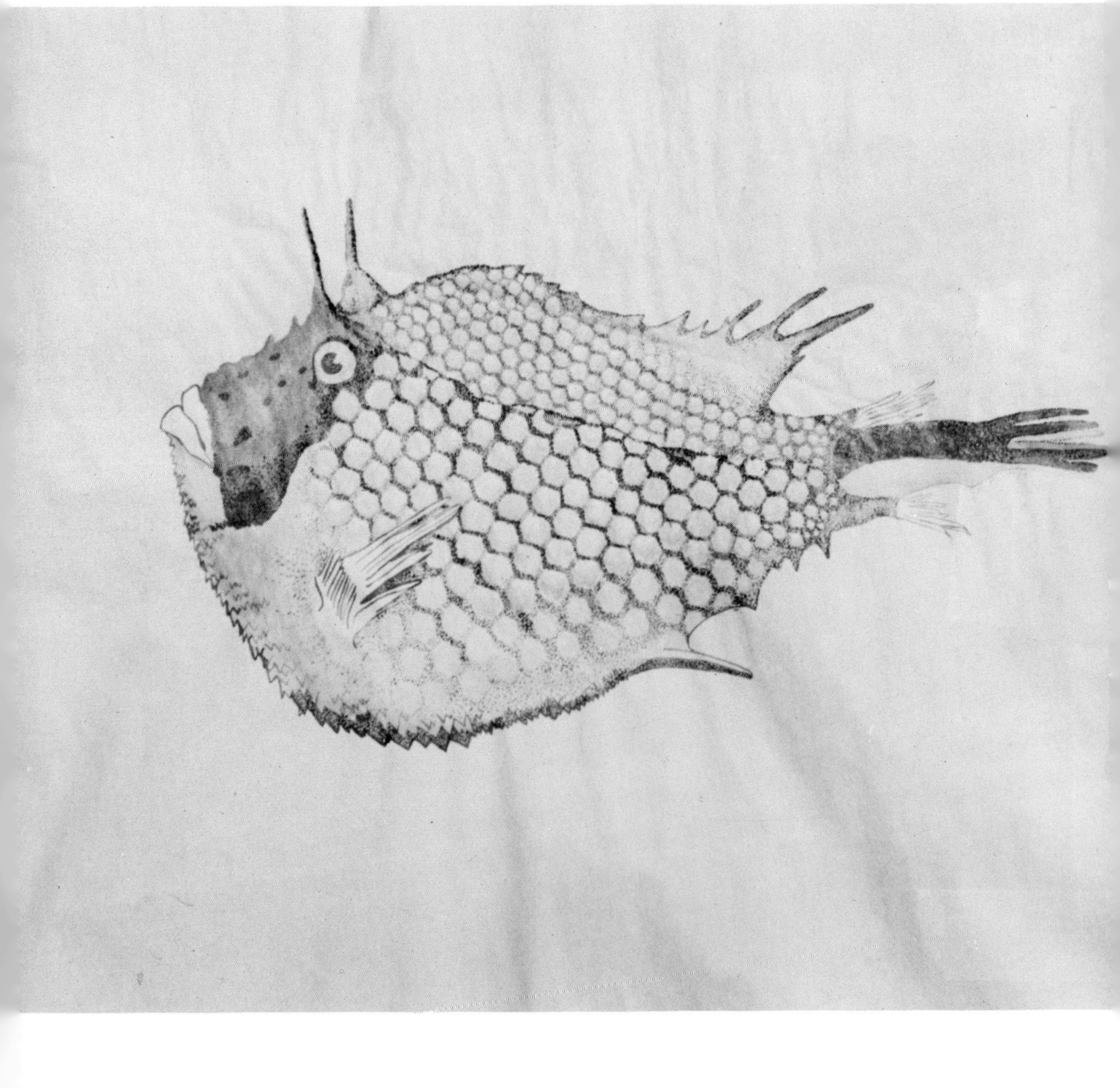

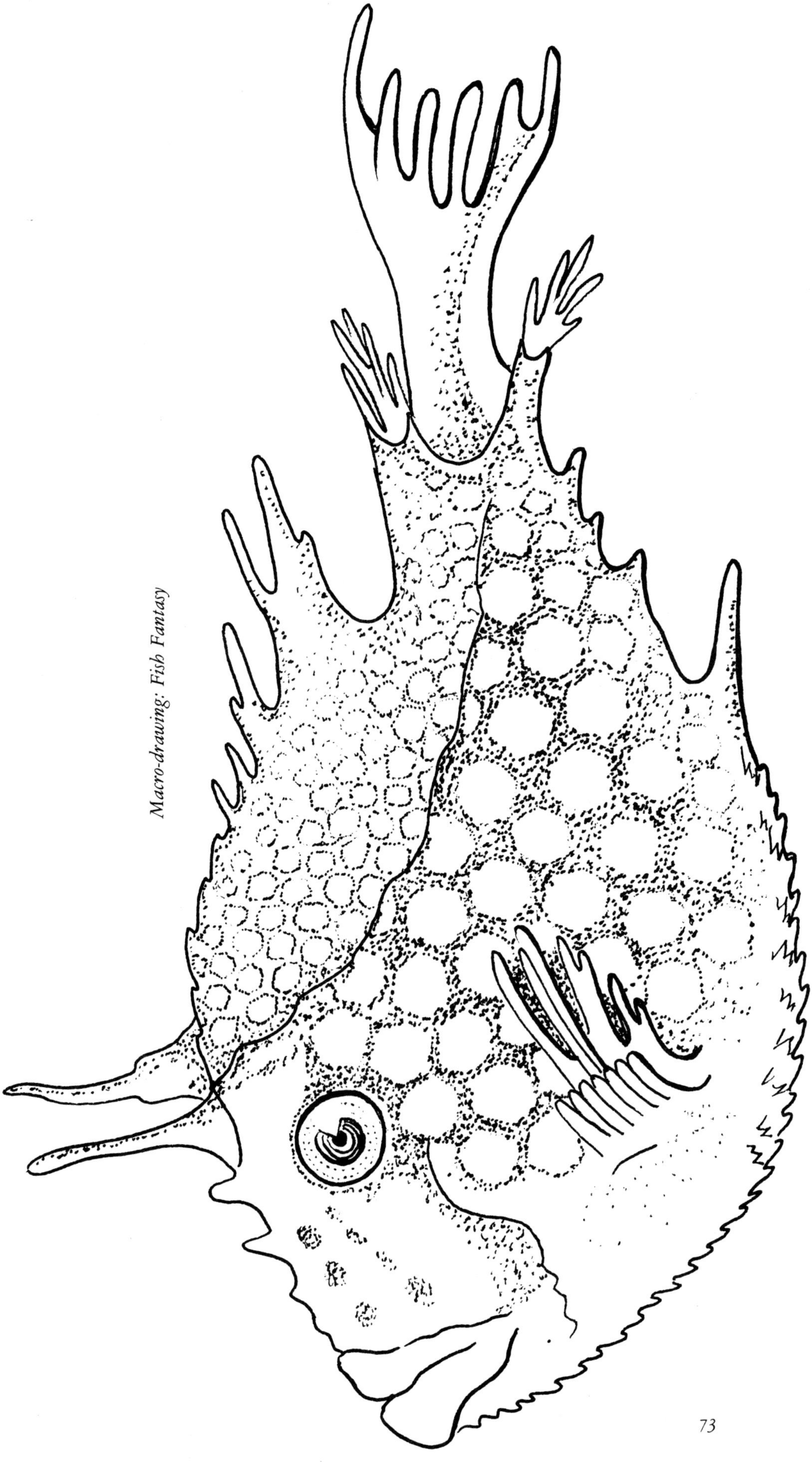

Macro-drawing: Fish Fantasy

PLACE MATS

Here is another way to use macro-designs. Large drawings may be laminated between two sheets of clear vinyl adhesive, which may be purchased from hardware and variety stores. This works best on drawings made on smooth lightweight illustration board. Add a border around the drawing with a permanent felt-tip pen. A good size for place mats is 12″ by 18″. Cut two pieces of vinyl this size and cut your drawing ½″ smaller on all sides than the adhesive vinyl.

Peel away the backing on one sheet of the vinyl and place it sticky side up. Carefully place the drawing ½″ from the border and, starting at one edge, smooth the drawing down. Next place the top adhesive vinyl over the back of the drawing, sticky side down. Press the edges of vinyl together. Smooth out any air bubbles. Trim the outer edges that do not meet properly.

Fish Drawing Place Mat (Designed by Kathy Poulsen)

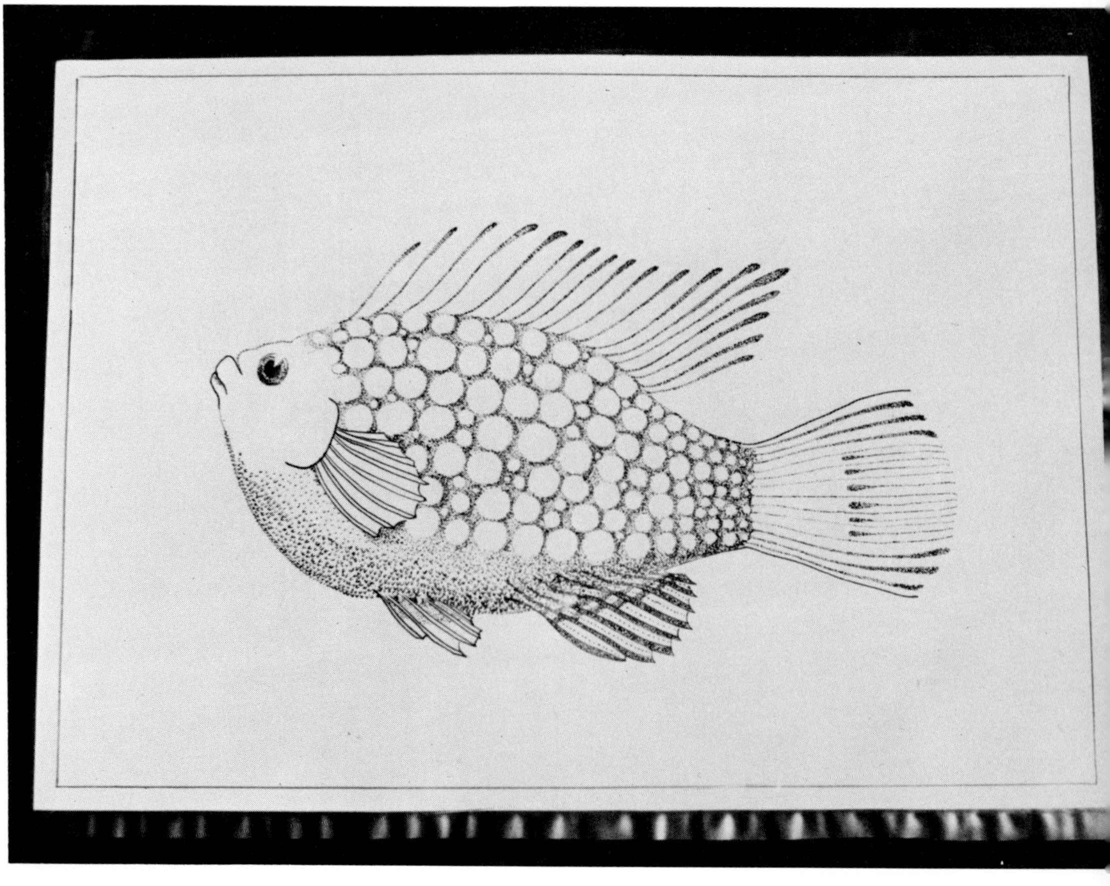

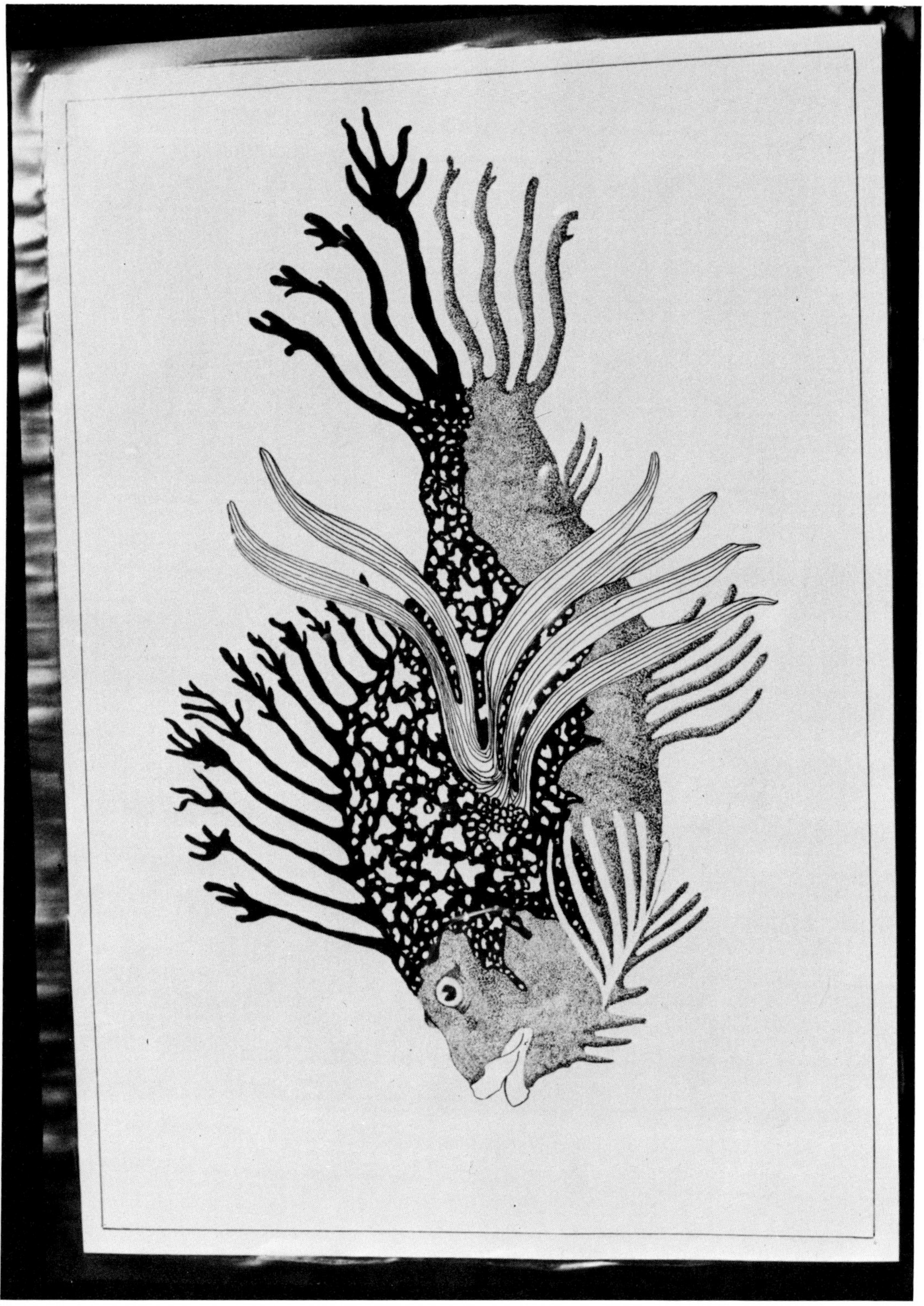

Fish Drawing Place Mat (Designed by Kathy Poulsen)

8
Designs for Children

Children love baby animal pictures. Shown here are some ways to use baby animal designs, but you may think of other projects on which to use the patterns.

BABY RACCOON

Brighten a child's room with a useful cork bulletin board. The design, painted with acrylics, is not harmed by pinning notes to it. You may have to use pressure in tracing the design onto the cork with carbon paper, but the acrylic paint will adhere easily.

Colors for the design are as follows: first a thin wash of yellow ocher is brushed on the background. Leaves are sketched with a pencil around the raccoon, then painted permanent green light, and outlined with raw umber. The dark areas of the raccoon are painted first with raw umber; next, a fine brush is used to stroke on lines of black, painting always in the direction of the fur growth. White highlights the eyes, nose, face, and ears. A few fine lines of white are stroked over the dark fur. No varnish is used.

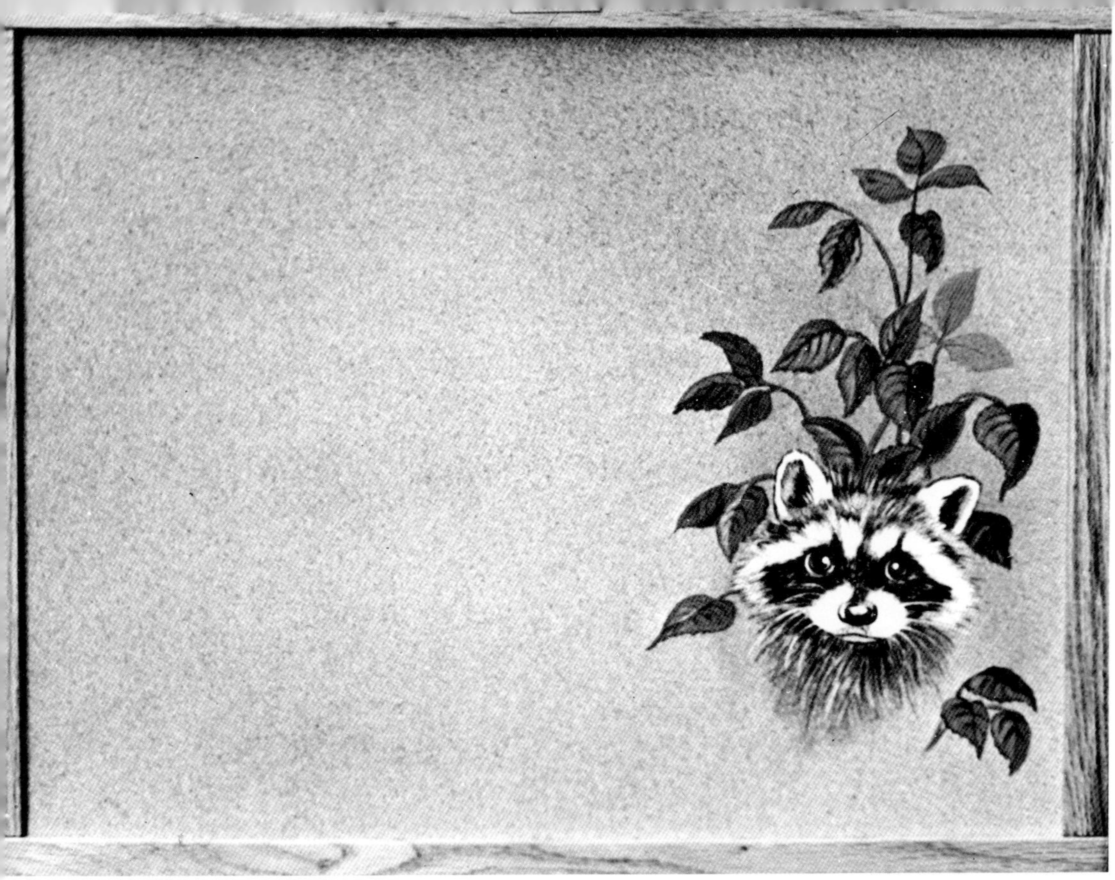

Baby Raccoon on Cork Bulletin Board

Baby Raccoon

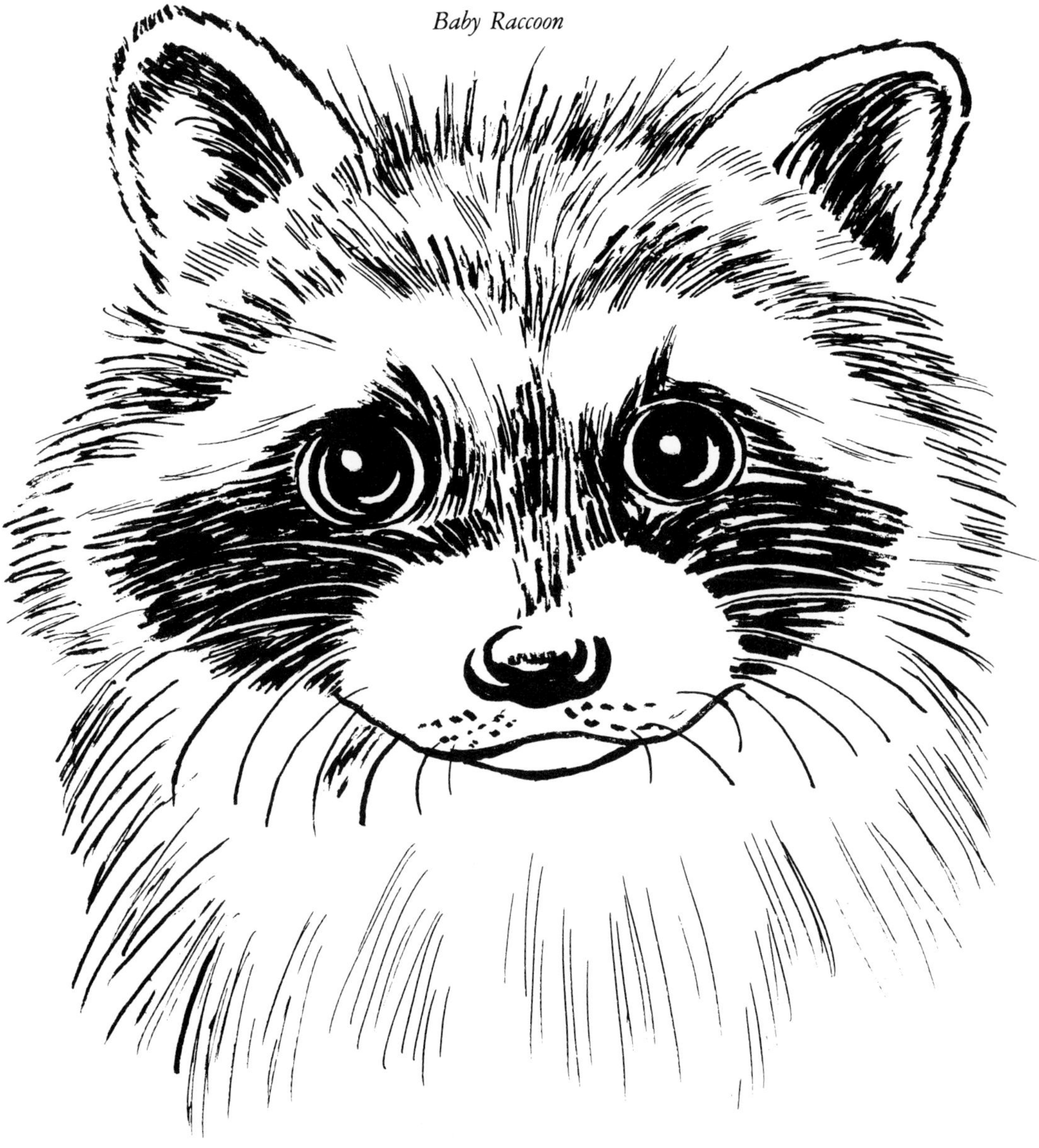

FAWN

Always a favorite with children, the fawn design can be used in many ways: wall plaques, children's furniture. Here it is applied to a child's barrel rocker.

The background is painted with permanent green light and shaded to cadmium yellow. When dry, the fawn design is traced with carbon paper. Colors for the fawn are burnt sienna, burnt umber, black, and white. The foliage of the ferns and a blossomed shrub are added freehand, using white and dark green (permanent green and black).

Varnish with polymer medium gloss for extra durability.

Fawn on Child's Rocker

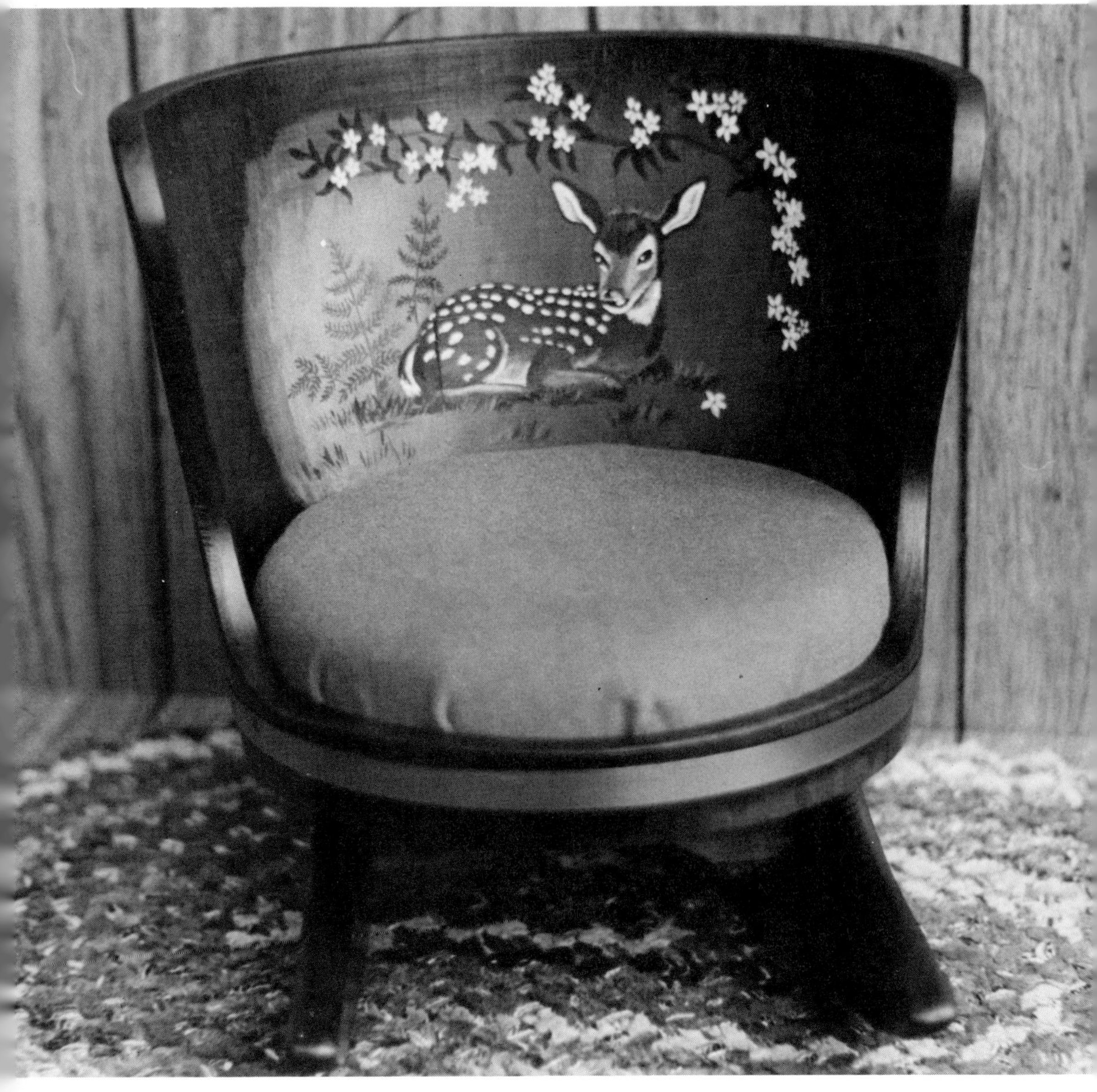

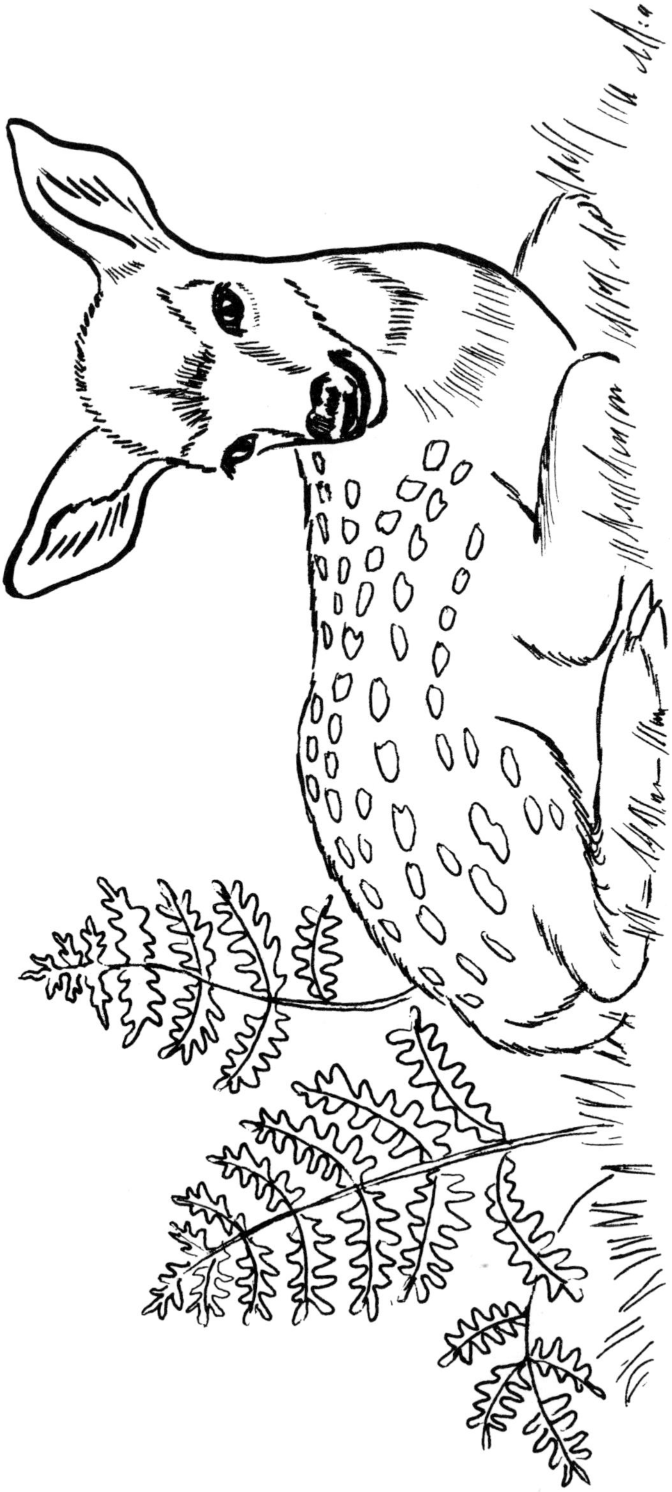

Fawn

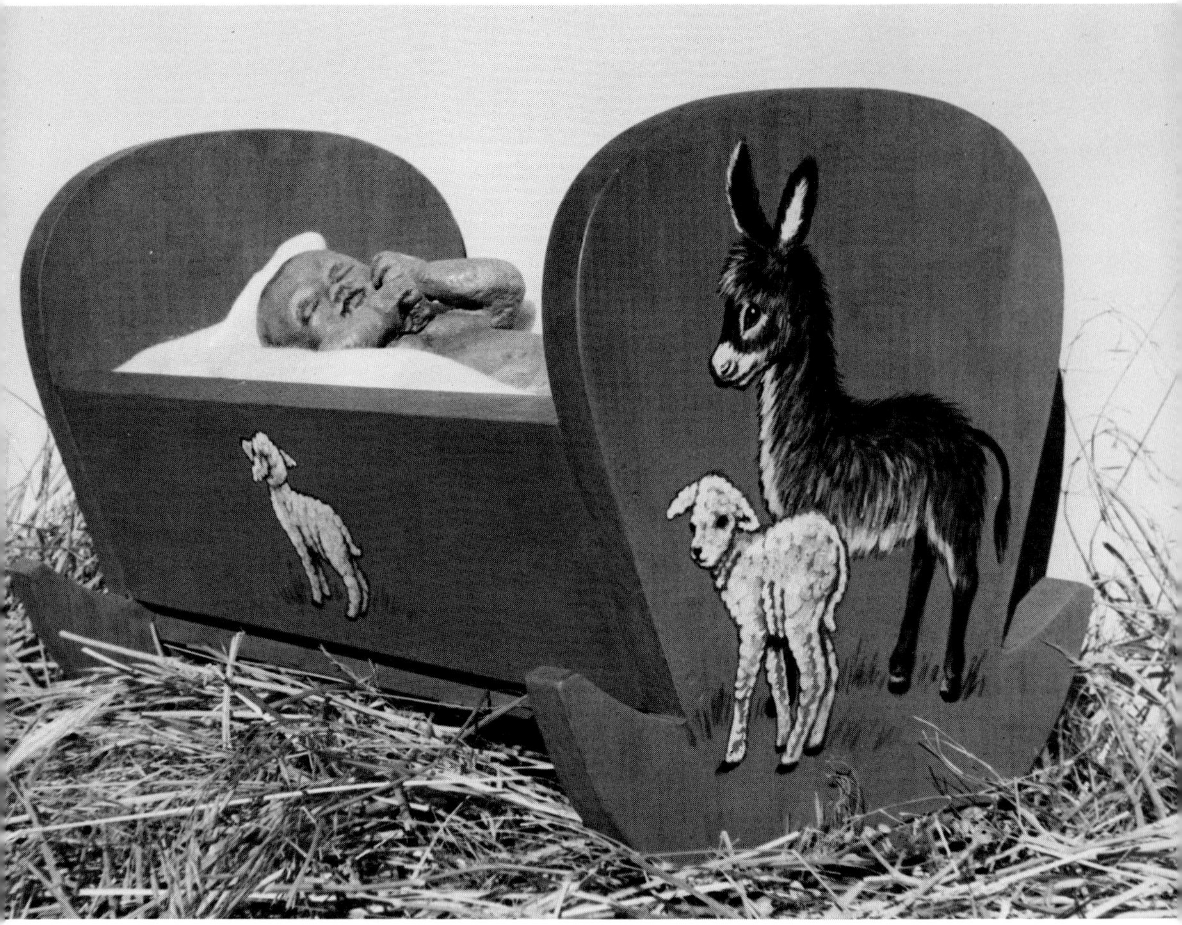

Lamb and Baby Donkey on Cradle

LAMBS AND BABY DONKEY

A doll's cradle may be used for an effective manger scene. Here the animals traditionally surrounding the manger crib are painted on the outside of the cradle.

Paint a base coat of yellow ocher using a water-thinned mixture and painting in the direction of the wood grain. When dry, trace on lambs and donkey. Outline the traced design with raw umber.

For a woolly lamb, dab on white with a round, pointed brush using a circular motion. Thin the white with water. The first coat will be dull. For the second coat, dab the white on full strength only where you want highlights.

The donkey is burnt umber. With rapid strokes of a small brush, paint the shaggy-looking fur. For the darker areas along the back and legs, add a little black.

No varnish is used.

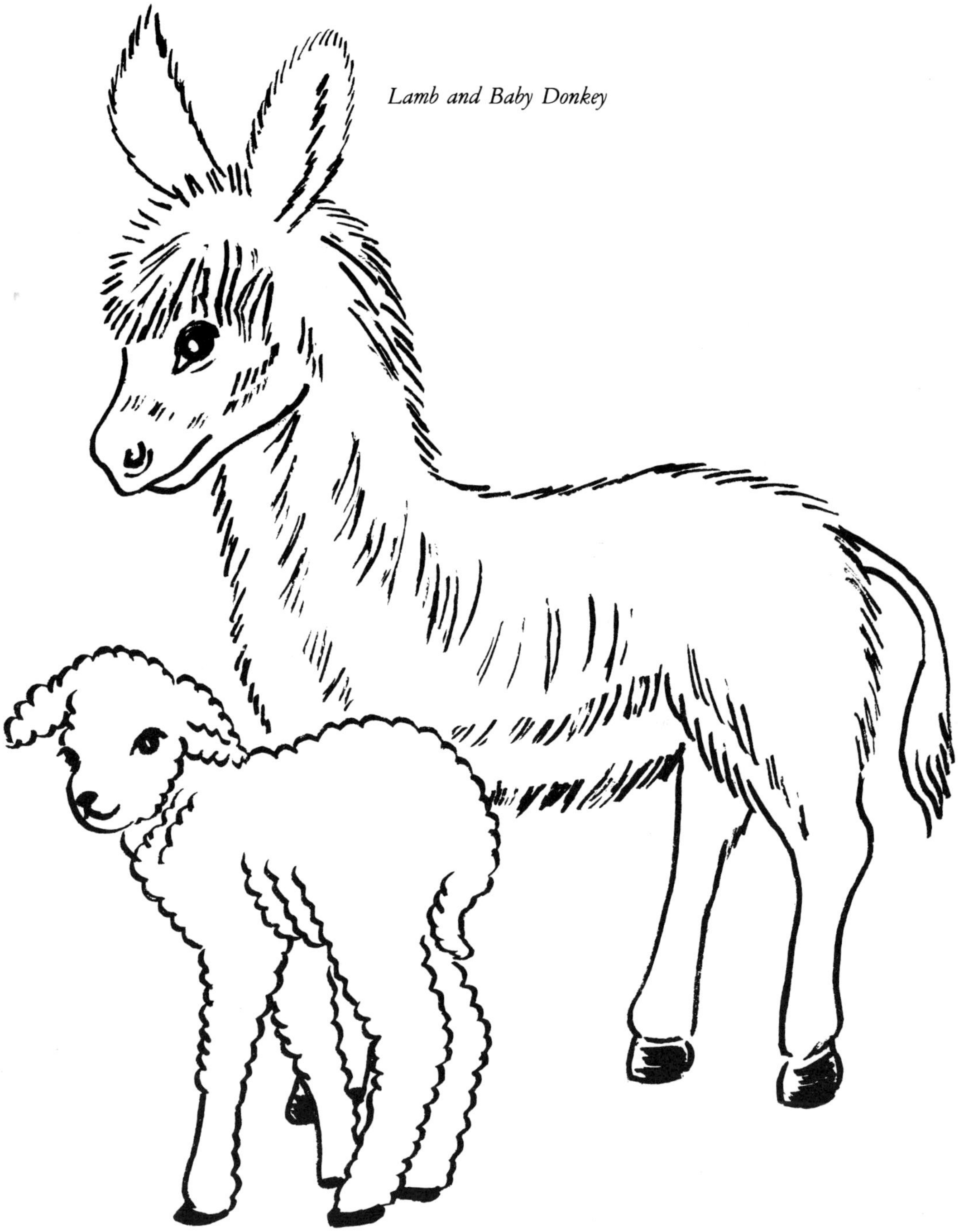

Lamb and Baby Donkey

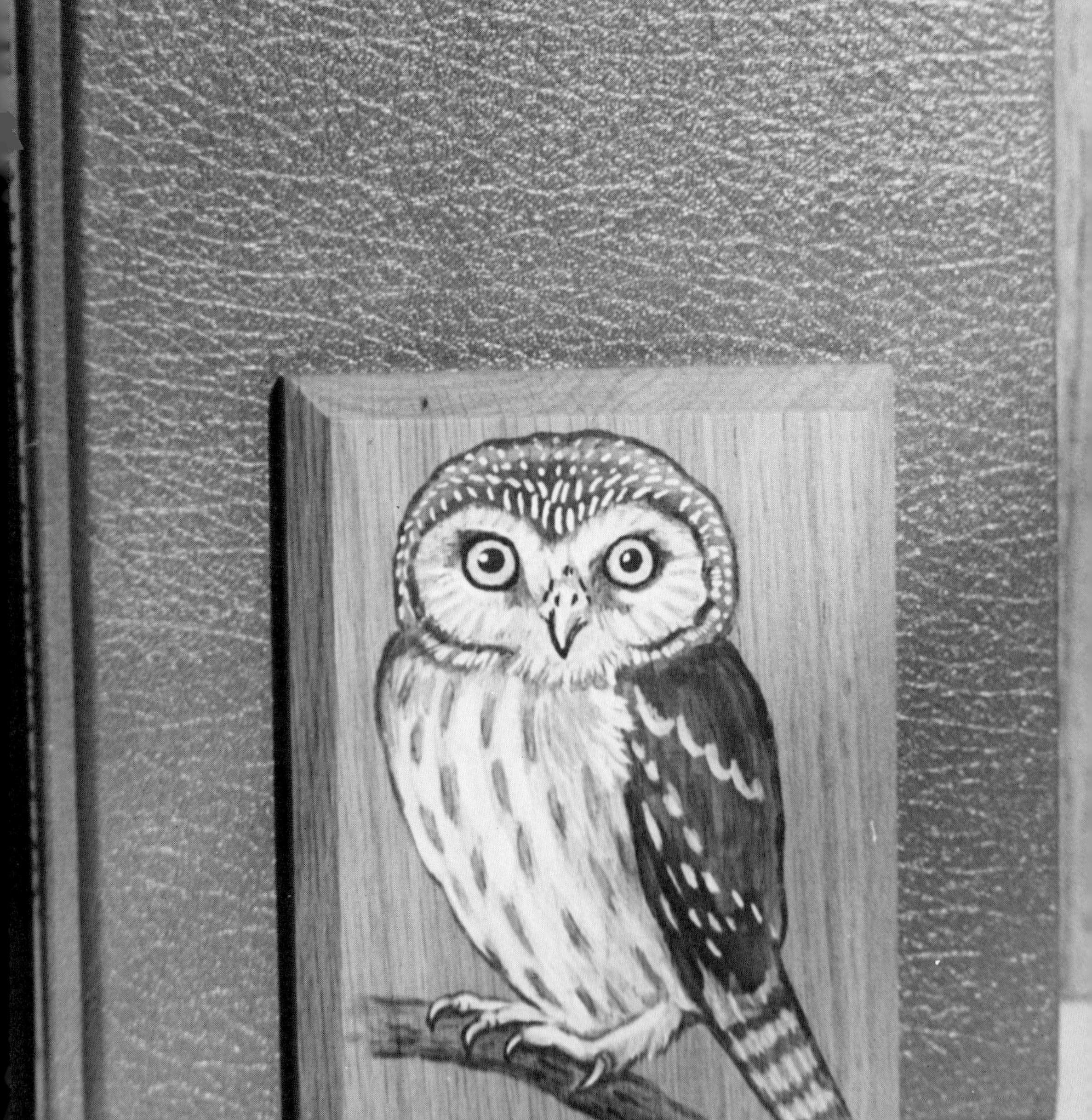

Pygmy Owl on Bookend

PYGMY OWL

The little owl on a bookend seems to say "Read Wisely." The design is painted directly onto the natural wood. If the bookends have been varnished, sand lightly with fine sandpaper so that the paint will adhere better.

Trace on the design. Outline with burnt umber. Paint the iris of the eyes with cadmium yellow, the pupils black, and add white highlights. Use white for facial feathers, beak, feet, and breast. The wings are burnt sienna and burnt umber. Burnt sienna darkens the top of the owl's head and accents the breast feathers. The tree branch is raw umber.

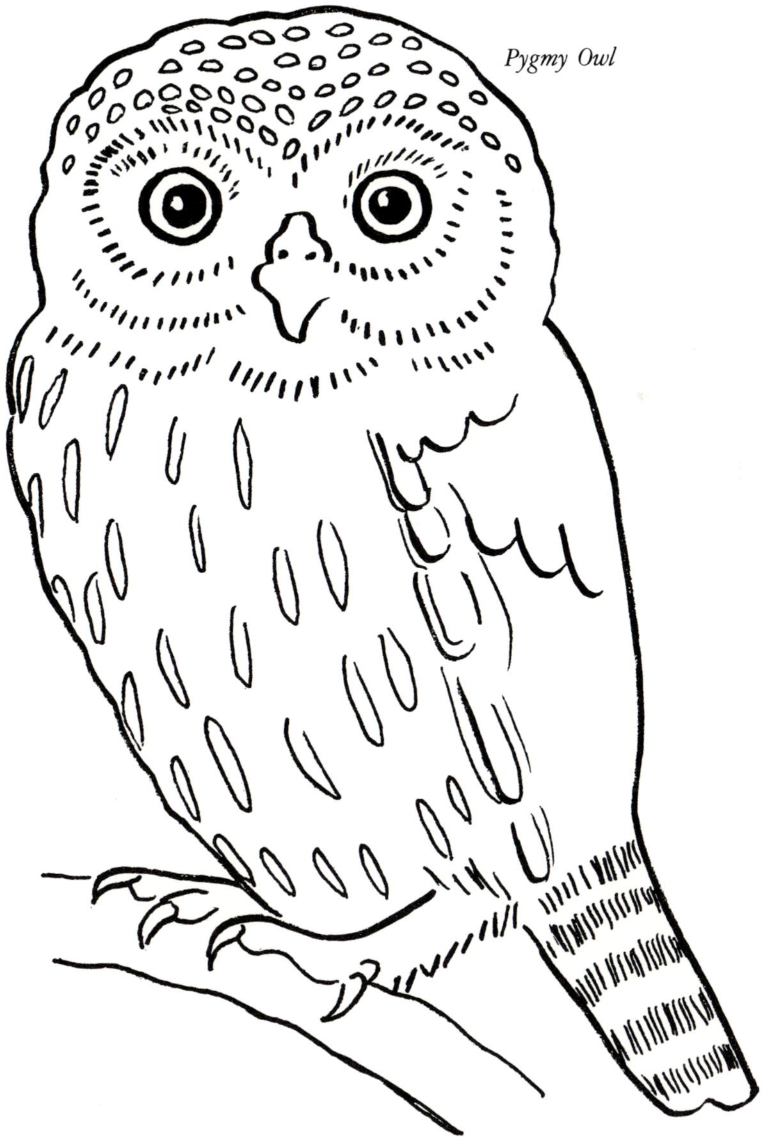

Pygmy Owl

BOBKITTENS IN A CAVE

Sand smooth a 10″ by 15″ plaque board and trace on the design. Outline the design with raw umber. The cave around the kittens is painted burnt sienna, then black, allowing some streaks of burnt sienna to show through.

The kitten's eyes are raw sienna with a thin wash of blue, pupils black, and white highlights. Shade the kittens with a thin wash of raw sienna. Brush on streaks of raw umber for the hair, and use black for spots. White accents the face, ears, breast, and tops of paws.

Rocks are suggested with a thin coloring of burnt sienna and gray. With a wad of paper towel, dip into a wash of burnt sienna and rub around the edges of the board, fading the color out toward the design. The sides and scalloped edge of the board are burnt umber.

Varnish with polymer medium gloss.

Bobkittens in a Cave

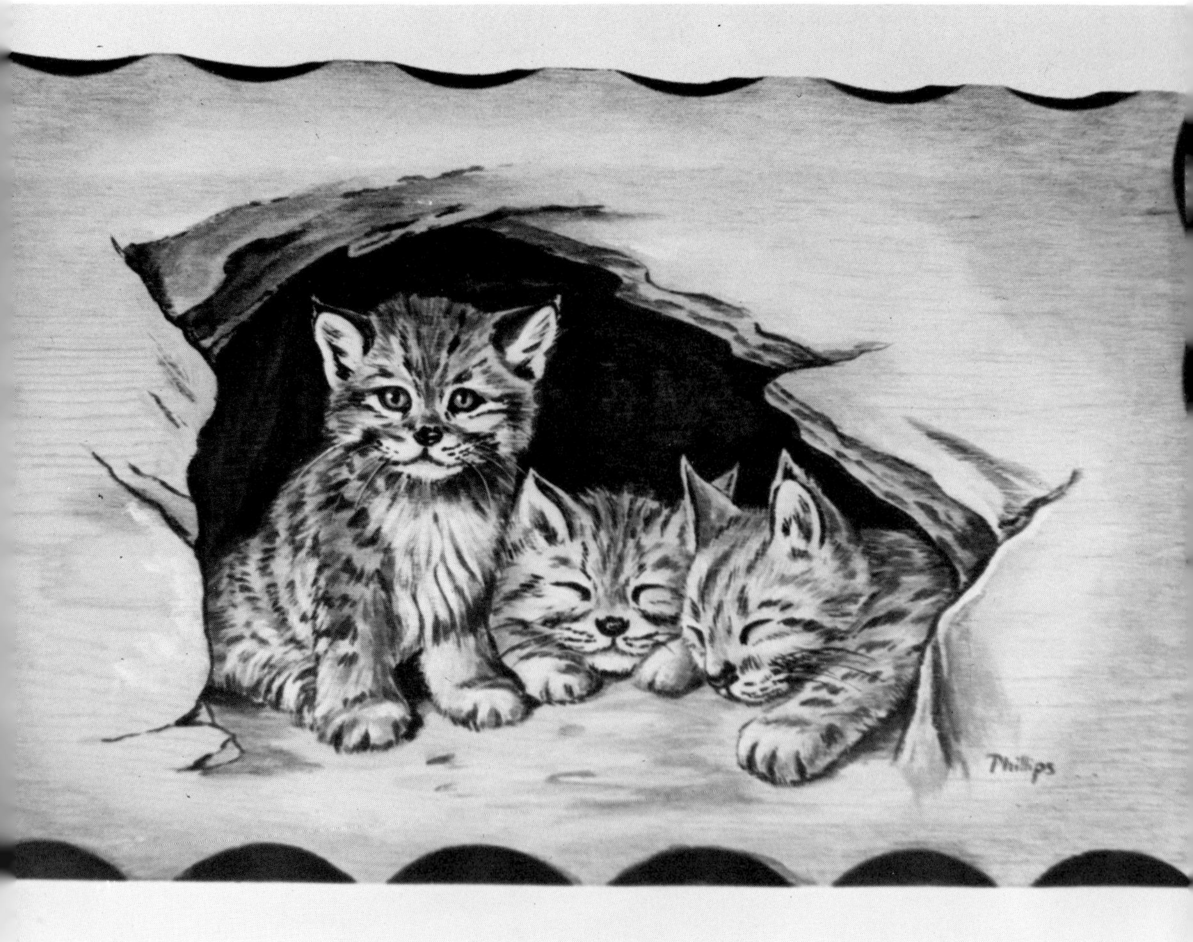

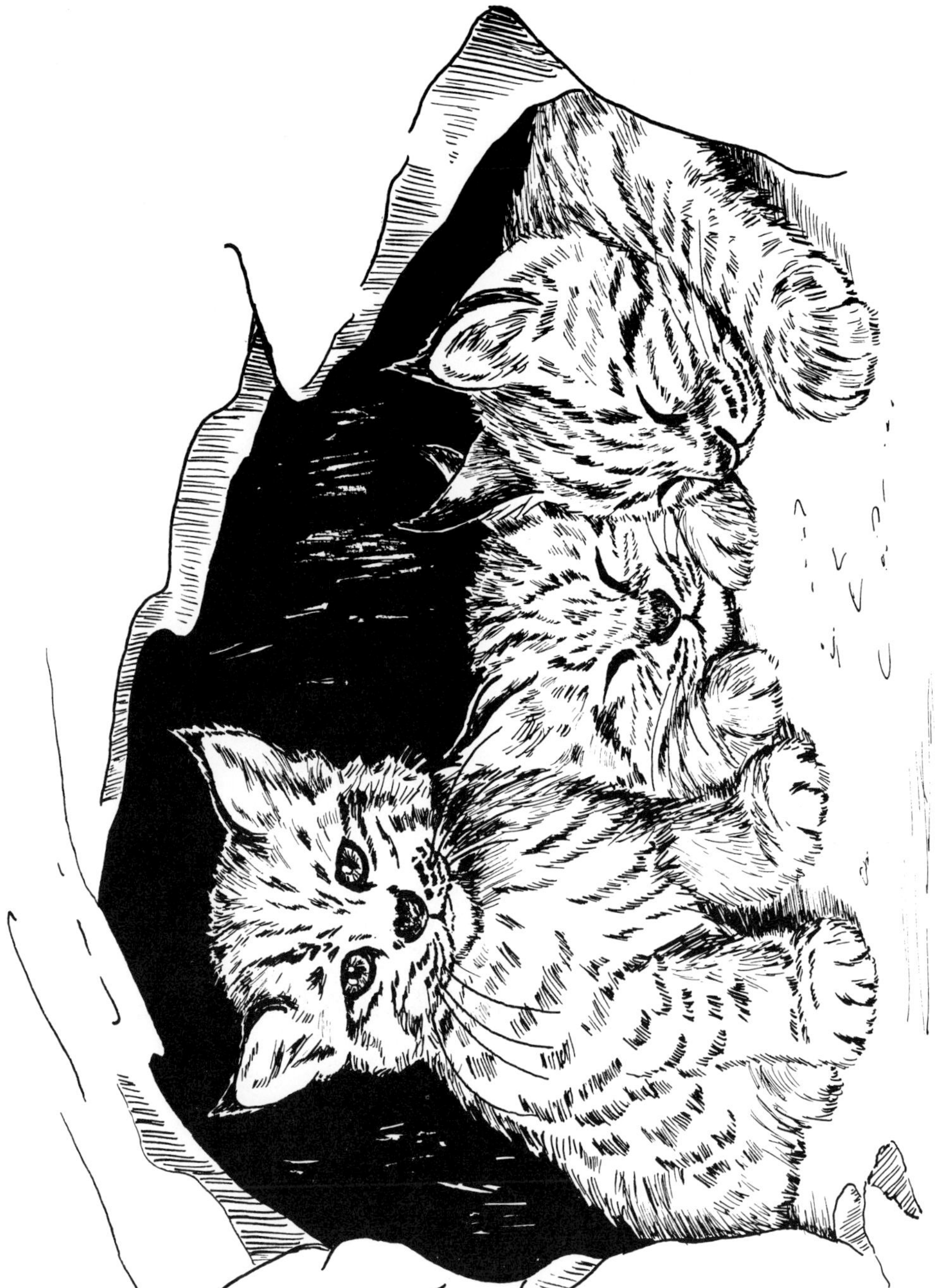

Bobkittens in a Cave

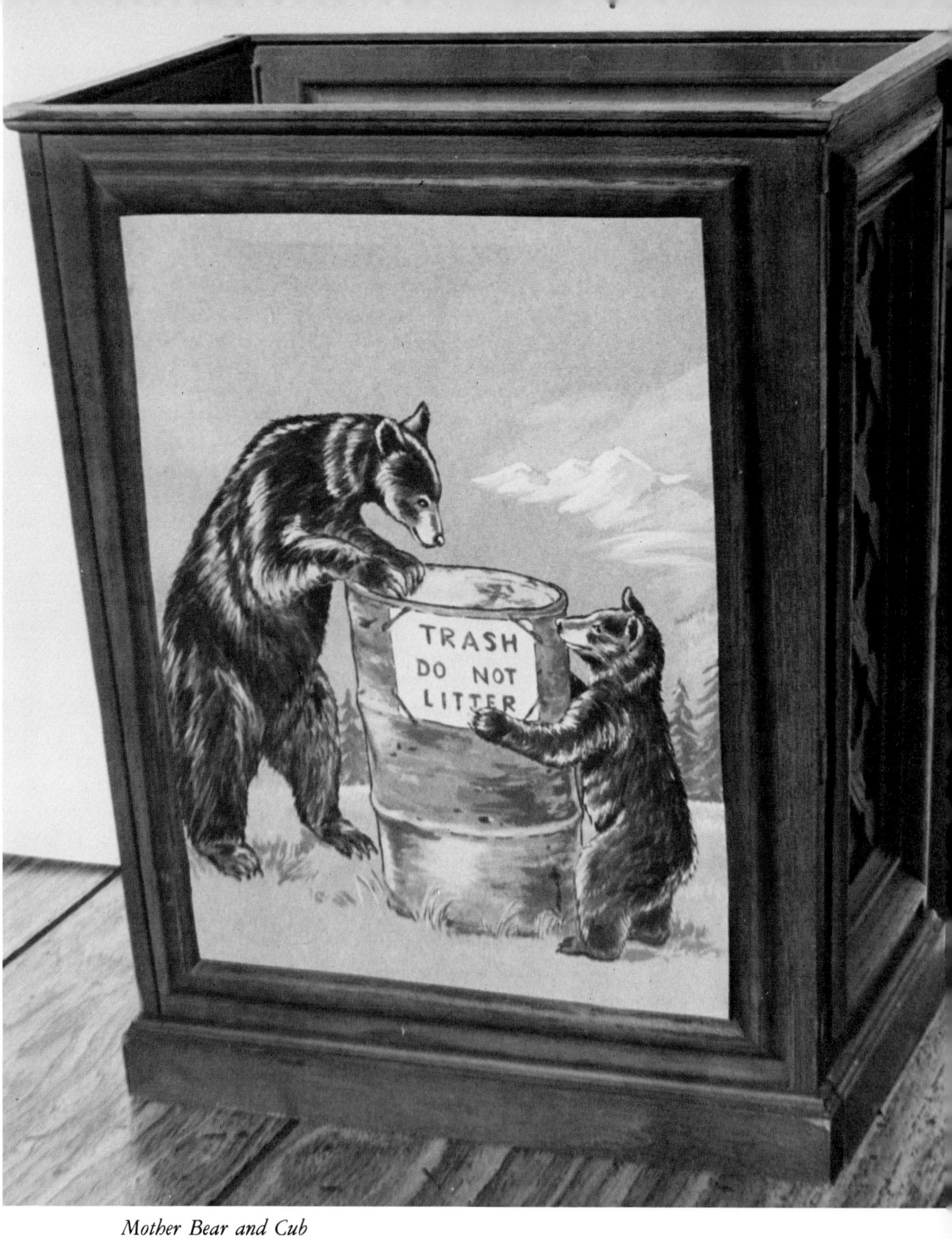

Mother Bear and Cub

MOTHER BEAR AND CUB

For a gentle reminder to children to keep their room tidy, use this bear design on a wastebasket.

Paint the bears with a water-thinned black first, using small strokes to suggest fur; then accent with full-strength black; add white highlights.

The rusty trash barrel is burnt sienna and raw umber outlined with black. Highlights are pale gray. Permanent green is used for grasses and trees.

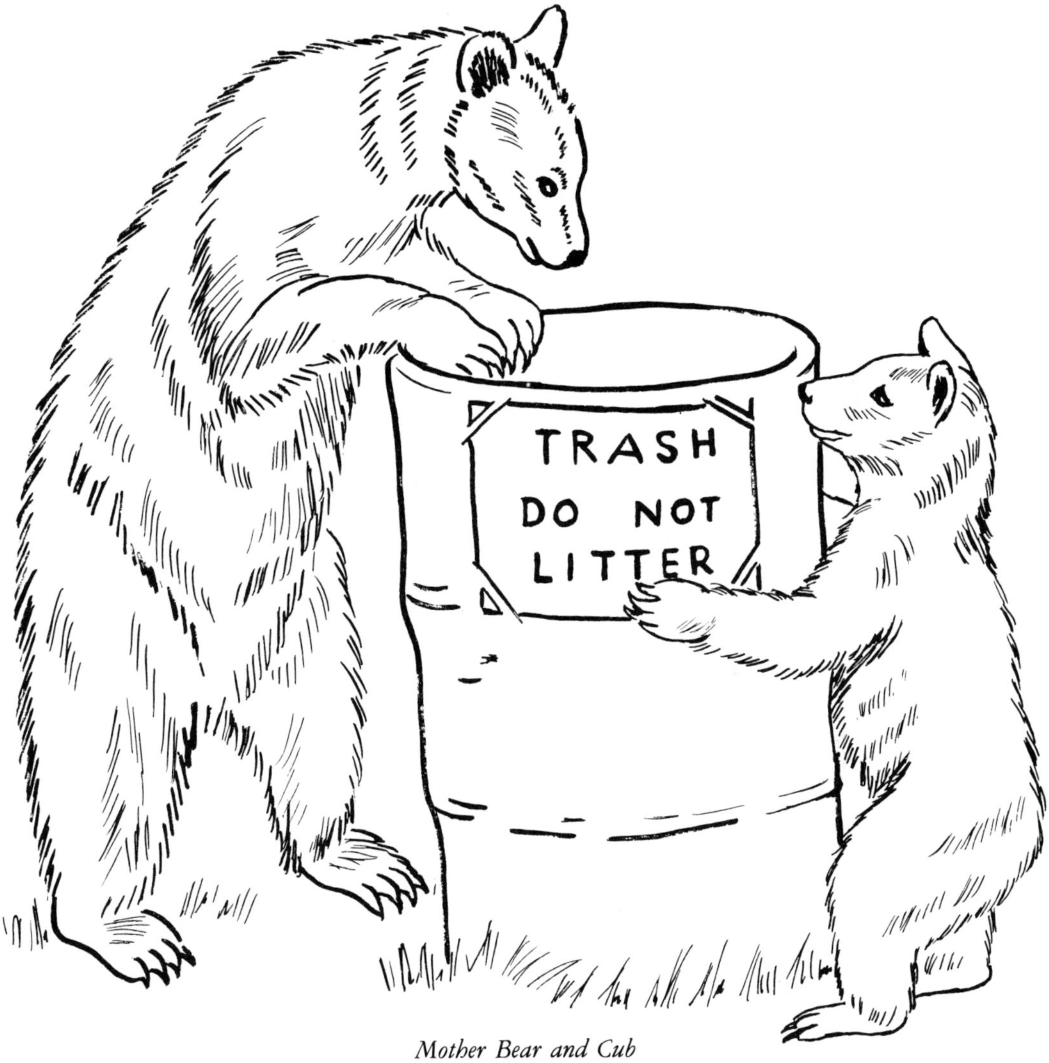

Mother Bear and Cub

BUTTERFLIES

To brighten a rainy day, add a few colorful butterflies to a clear plastic umbrella. Shown here are two butterflies to add a colorful note, but small enough so that vision through the umbrella is not obstructed.

It is easy to paint a design on clear plastic. Open the umbrella and tape the pattern face down on the outside. On the inside trace the design with a small brush dipped in black acrylic. Fill in the design with bright yellow for the large butterfly and orange for the smaller one. Since the butterflies are painted on the inside of the umbrella they will likely withstand the stormiest weather.

Butterflies

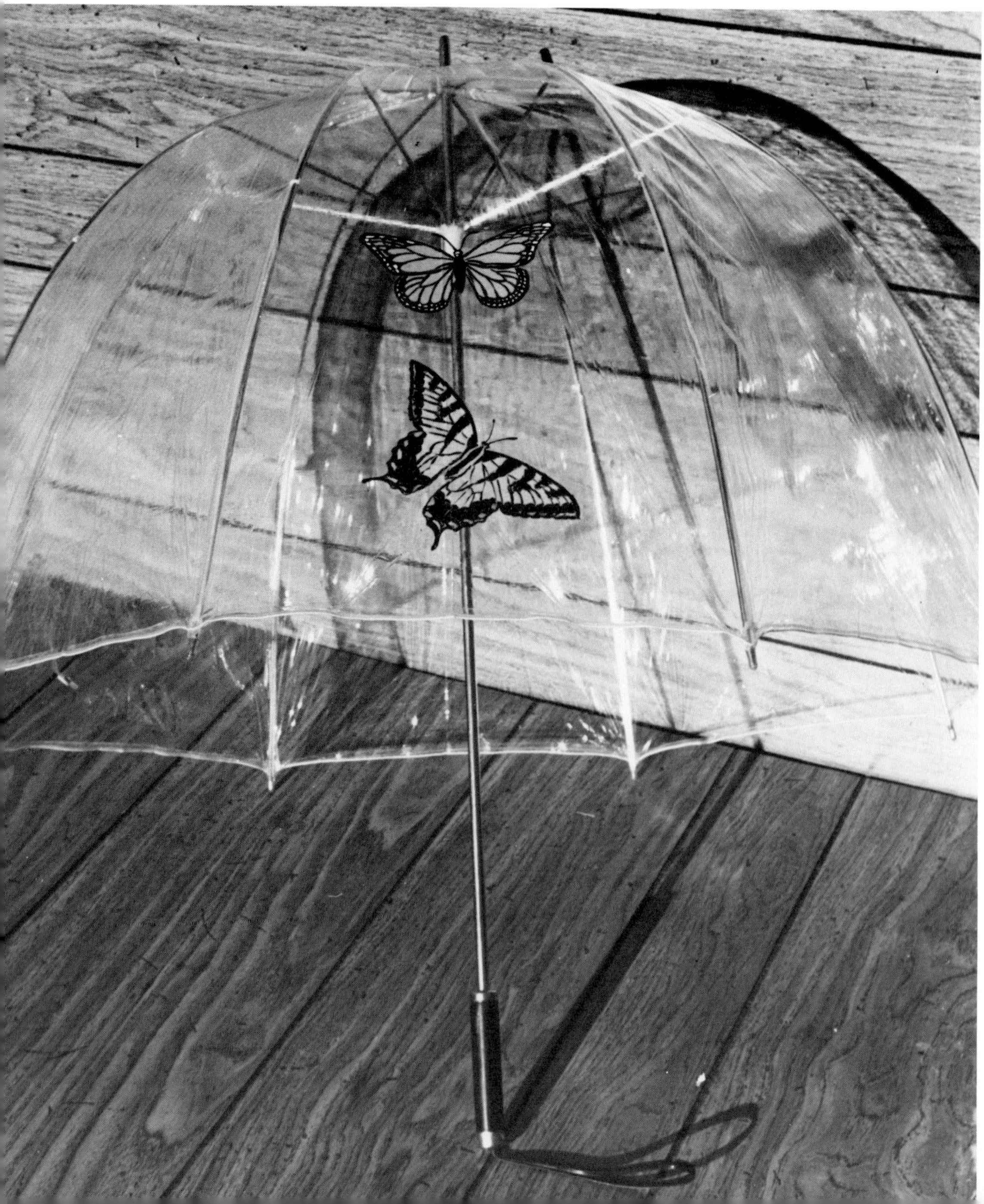

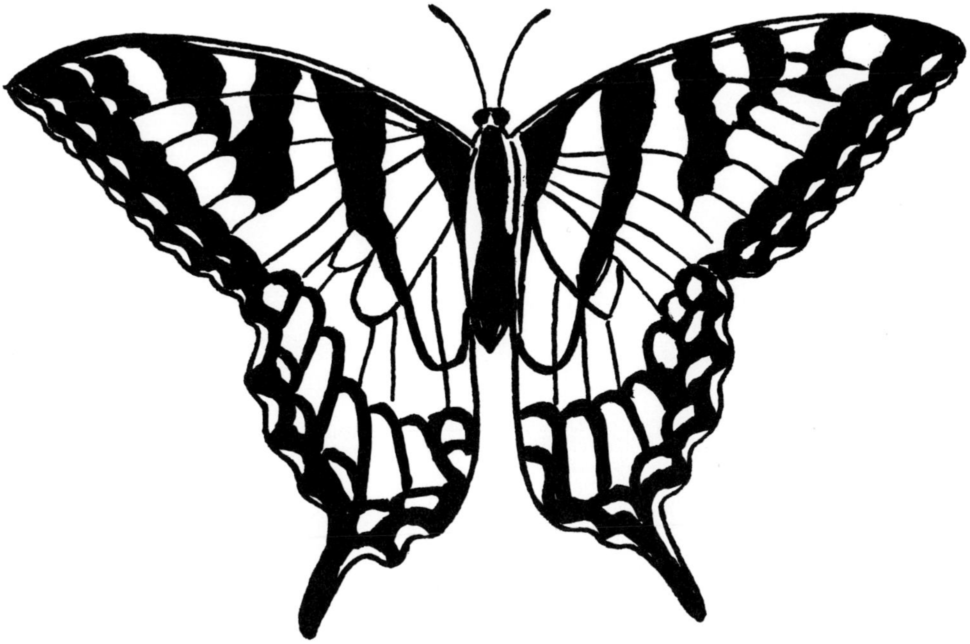

Butterflies

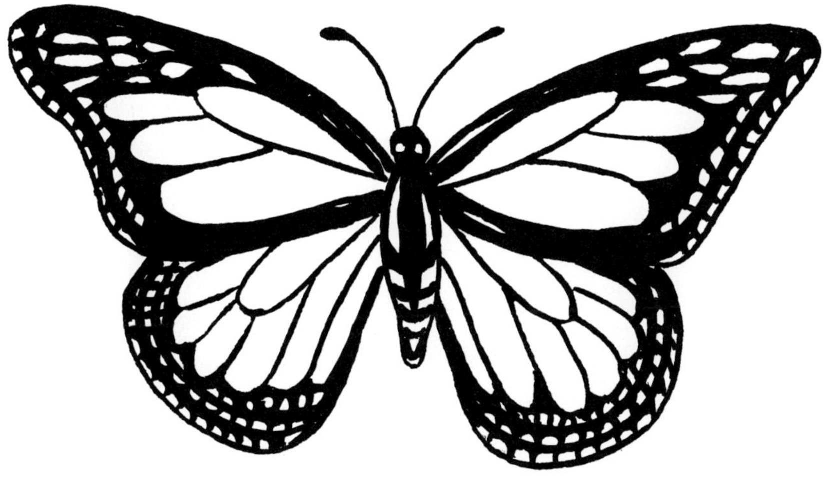

9
Enlarging a Design

You may want a larger or smaller design than you find in this book. If so, here is an easy method of changing the size of any design.

First trace the original design onto a piece of tracing paper. With a ruler divide the traced design into equal squares.

Now on a separate paper mark off the same number of squares either smaller or larger in size. It will be helpful to number each square up and across matching numbers with the squares on the original design.

Fill in each square with the part of the design shown in the corresponding square.

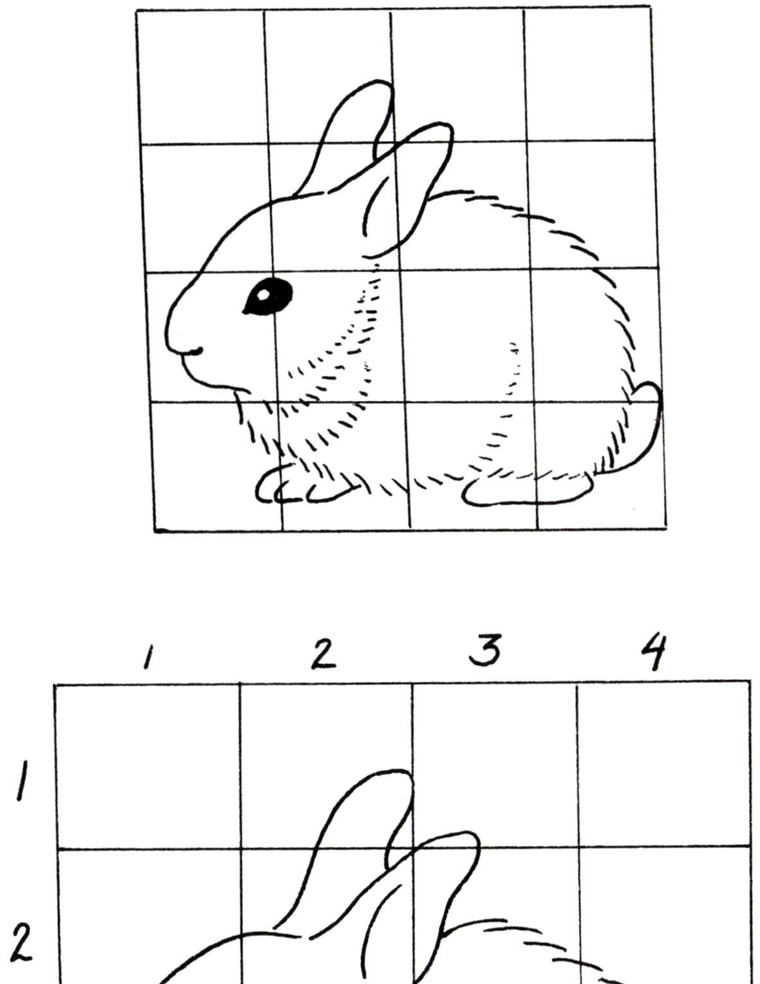

Enlarging a Design

For Further Reading

Adams, E. "Macro-Drawing from Nature." *School Arts Magazine,* November 1966.

Downer, M. *Discovering Design.* New York: Lothrop, Lee and Shepard Co., 1947.

Feininger, A. *The Anatomy of Nature.* New York: Crown Publishers, Inc., 1956.

Haeck, E. *Art Forms in Nature.* New York: Dover Publications, Inc., 1974.

Horst, H. P. *Patterns from Nature.* Locust Valley, New York: J. J. Augustine, 1946.

Parker, X. L. *Designing for Crafts.* New York: Charles Scribner's Sons, 1974.

Proctor, R. M. *The Principles of Pattern.* New York: Van Nostrand Reinhold Company, 1969.

Scheffer, V. *The Seeing Eye.* New York: Charles Scribner's Sons, 1971.

Index